A Practical Guide to
Project
Management

How to Make it Work in Your Organisation

Celia Burton and
Norma Michael

KOGAN
PAGE

For those people whose lives are touched by the
management of change

First published in New Zealand as *Basic Project Management* by Reed
Books, a division of Octopus Publishing Group, in 1991

This edition published by Kogan Page, London, in 1992
Reprinted 1993

Kogan Page Limited
120 Pentonville Road
London N1 9JN

British Library Cataloguing in Publication Data
A CIP record for this book is available from the British Library.

ISBN 0 7494 07905

Printed in England by Clays Ltd., St Ives plc

Acknowledgments

Many people have helped in the international research for, and production of this book. We would like to thank Steve Miller for his interest and advice, Chris Comber for his help with the computer side of things, John Culliford, Paul Bayliss, Lyn Little, Don Hunn, Rob Laking, Doug Martin, Paul Carpenter, Reg Hammond, Robin Darling, Nickie Jones, Gillian Biscoe, Roger Blakeley, Steven Vaughan, Dennis Bushking, Christina Wells, Neil Fyfe, Norman McKenzie, Gordon Rabey, Ray Michael, J P Michael, Eric Van Helmond, Gordon Michael, Ron Ritchie, Gary McKay, Paula Keene, Barbara Roberts, Peter Davies, Peter Shaw, Graham Bennett, David Haig, Craig Sparrow, Peter Millar, Tim Carter, R H Neale, Elizabeth Cartwright.

Thanks to the many organisations that gave assistance, especially Loughborough University, Salisbury's, East Hampshire Council, Clwyd Alyn, the Association of Project Managers, the Housing Corporation of New Zealand for permission to use part of their training video script by Dell King; the Ministry of the Environment for their permission to adapt Figures 4, 5 and 6 on pages 12–15; The International Labour Organisation, Geneva, for permission to use their Control diagram on page 92; and to GP Books for permission to quote from Frank Sligo's *Conflict Management* on page 48.

In particular we would like to express our indebtedness and appreciation to Linda Cassells and Chris Price, our editors, for their perception and help.

Introduction

The typical large business 20 years hence will have fewer than half the levels of management of its counterpart today, and no more than a third the managers .... Because of its flatter structure, the large, information-based organisation will more closely resemble the businesses of a century ago than today's big companies. Back then, however, all the knowledge, such as it was, lay with the very top people. The rest were helpers or hands, who mostly did the same work and did as they were told. In the information-based organisation, the knowledge will be primarily at the bottom, in the minds of the specialists who do different work and direct themselves.

> Peter Drucker
> *Harvard Business Review*
> 1988

Business today is in transition. The restructuring that Peter Drucker talks about has already begun. People in organisations are being told to run with it. As the organisations change, people who can't adapt, go. Those who stay may be pulled out of their familiar niches because of their knowledge and told they are now going to be working on a team project. People previously directed from above are increasingly being made responsible for:

- Gathering the information they need
- Disseminating information
- Developing self-control mechanisms within their team to ensure their objectives are being met.

If you are such a person, you are having to change some old habits and acquire new ones. To be more specific, you are having to learn a wide range of new skills which come under the umbrella of **Organisational Project Management,** a term still new to some of the people involved in or affected by project management. In this new business environment you may feel yourself to be more visible, and the results you achieve may be more readily assessed.

Traditional project management originated in the construction industry. It is a comparative newcomer in business organisations. Making project management work in your business organisation is the subject of this book. So, whether you are new to project management or keen to learn more about it, our intention is to provide you with basic guidelines on how to get started on projects, and how to see projects through to a satisfactory conclusion.

Many readily available books explain the theory of project management — the **what,** as we see it. We want to go a step further, to explain the **how.** If you are unsure of the pitfalls of project management or don't know where to begin, then the guidelines, techniques and strategies that follow should help. You may be the only person responsible for managing the project, or you may be a team leader or a member of a team within an organisation. No matter what your role, this guide to project management provides you with a basic framework for that special job. Regard it as your toolkit in project management. If you are a project manager, encourage your project team to read it so that they too understand how a project is set up, how you identify resource requirements and how you meet those needs.

The need that we identified while working with people engaged in projects, and that prompted us to write this book, was based on the claims of many that they did not understand the principles or techniques of project management, or could not see how project management could be made to fit into their organisations.

This book is our response. It is for people coping with change, of which achieving objectives by means of projects, small or large, is an integral part.

If we can help you further in any way, or if you have comments or contributions based on your own experience that we could use in future editions of this book, we'd be happy to hear from you. You can reach us through the publishers.

*To succeed is to leave the world a bit
better by a job well done*
Ralph Waldo Emerson

PART 1

*P*HASE ONE: WHAT YOU NEED TO KNOW AND DO TO SET UP A PROJECT

Contents

List of figures

Overview of techniques and strategies

WHEN IS IT A PROJECT?

Call it what you like, work is work.

True, but in project management terms, a project is work that has a beginning and an end. It is planned and controlled; it can be brought to a successful conclusion; it creates change. Ongoing work such as dealing with incoming mail is not a project, but reorganising the process of how incoming mail is handled is a project.

Some examples of projects are:

- Planning a training session or conference
- Refurbishing an office
- Managing a computer installation programme
- Moving office
- Organising social club functions
- Introducing new service
- Making changes to a management structure or processes.

You may not yet have been a project manager or even a member of a project team, but we believe it is very likely that as an employee you will already have been affected by the consequences of a project at some time in your business life, whether it was to do with office layout or computer access.

Projects range widely in size and complexity. However, what is not so obvious is that certain procedures are common to all of them. All projects may be planned and carried out in the following four phases (see Figure 1):

Pre-planning

This is probably the most important phase in the whole project. Here you determine what has to be done and whether it should be done at all. The feasibility of the project is checked at all phases. In pre-planning you create a workable environment for the project.

Detailed planning

The tasks, resources, effects and needs of the project are examined in depth.

Implementation, monitoring and controlling

The person or team carries out the work according to the plan.

Post-project review

The whole project is reviewed. Information is gathered for records to help people undertaking projects in the future.

TYPES OF PROJECT AND BASIC PROCEDURE

Projects range from the simple single project to a number of interlinked complex projects. They can last for a few days or a few years. The work content of every project varies. The basic procedure, however, remains the same. The relatively simple planning of a two-day seminar requires **planning** and **coordination.** It has to be done within a set **time. Estimates** and **budgets** have to be prepared, and the work has to be **monitored** and **controlled.** Advice and cooperation may be sought from people not directly involved, but, essentially, one person is responsible for achieving results and for the quality of those results.

PROJECT PHASES

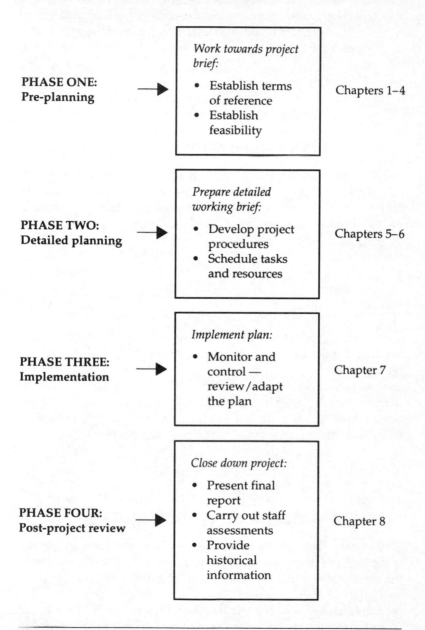

PHASE ONE:
Pre-planning

Work towards project brief:

- Establish terms of reference
- Establish feasibility

Chapters 1–4

PHASE TWO:
Detailed planning

Prepare detailed working brief:

- Develop project procedures
- Schedule tasks and resources

Chapters 5–6

PHASE THREE:
Implementation

Implement plan:

- Monitor and control — review/adapt the plan

Chapter 7

PHASE FOUR:
Post-project review

Close down project:

- Present final report
- Carry out staff assessments
- Provide historical information

Chapter 8

Figure 1

The same basic procedure applies to more complex work such as reviewing corporate structures and procedures, but the major difference here will probably be the need for a wider range of skills. As more staff or consultants come into the project and more tasks have to be coordinated, the projects become harder to control.

PROJECT MANAGEMENT

Our definition of project management is the process by which the project manager plans and controls the tasks within the projects and the resources on which the organisation draws to carry out the projects. By 'resources' we mean:

- People
- Money
- Equipment
- Time.

Project management is a skilful use of techniques to achieve the required results to a set standard, within a budget and within a certain time.

Bringing a project to a successful conclusion relates directly to management by objectives, that is, it measures its success by the degree to which it achieves the objectives set. Project management helps to ensure success in meeting objectives.

PROJECT MANAGEMENT TECHNIQUES

Project management techniques are part of the **how** in getting any project off the ground. A project manager, and also possibly the members of a project team, will be involved in:

- **Scheduling** — breaking the project down into a series of tasks; estimating durations and resources and linking them in a logical way

- **Managing** — leading, coaching, supporting, making decisions; achieving results through other people's efforts (except on a one-person project)
- **Coordinating** — ensuring different parts of the work are brought together efficiently; identifying links across other work areas
- **Monitoring and controlling** — dealing with the changes that occur during the project (outside the ultimate change the project is designed to bring about).

You will need to monitor and control what is being done to ensure that the project is staying on track, or alter and amend the plan to take into account any new requirements. You keep track of the project tasks and resources by means of reports, communication strategies and scheduling techniques.

PROJECT STRATEGIES

Project strategies are what make the wheels turn smoothly.

Policy guidelines

These are the general instructions needed by organisations that run several projects. They are written specifically for the organisation concerned.

Procedures

Procedures are set up to facilitate the dissemination of information to all concerned. They provide easy access for input, when necessary, from people within the organisation or outside it.

Ground rules

Agreement and understanding of what is acceptable behaviour within working groups or teams is essential. For example, the ground rules set out the duration of meetings, and state how soon after a meeting the minutes are to be circulated. Important topics such as specific requirements for peer evaluation of any papers prepared by individual members of the team should also be included. These ground rules are sometimes set after the team has assembled, or they may appear in the policy guidelines. They are mentioned again in Chapter 5.

Communication and feedback strategies

These are essential for any project, but especially so for a complex organisation that has several projects running simultaneously. Choose the method that suits the project (see page 98).

THE PEOPLE OFFICIALLY INVOLVED

In the case of a large project, the project manager requires the support of other people, who would fit into a project hierarchy which may be made up in a number of ways. Figure 2 shows one possible structure.

No matter whether the project is large or small, the person responsible for the project needs to encourage the visible support of at least one member of senior management. The reasons are discussed in Chapter 2.

A core team sometimes assists in the pre-planning phase of a project before the project team is selected. The core team is involved because of their core skills (such as administration) and knowledge of the job in hand.

Project hierarchies appear to be the norm in organisations which operate on a project management basis, with each level assigned a clearly defined role. These roles are discussed in detail in Chapter 4.

DEALING WITH ORGANISATIONAL CHANGE

We've already established that projects by their nature create change. One project may create other projects. Being forewarned, you can be prepared for chain reactions and plan accordingly.

One outcome of these chain reactions is that organisations may, without having planned for the change, turn from a traditional line environment (where managers control their own

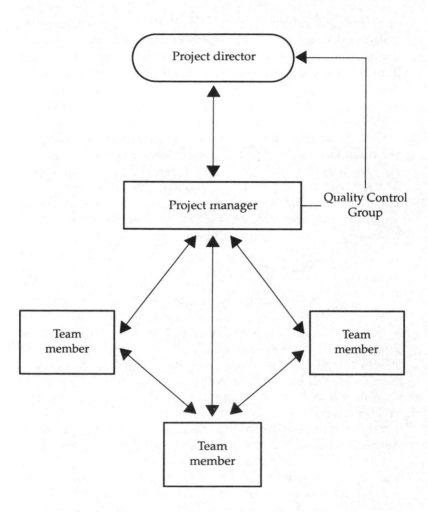

Figure 2

divisional ongoing work — see Figure 3) to management by projects (a new game where the old rules no longer apply).

Existing work structures and resource requirements may crumble as staff begin to be used in a different way. They may now have to report to more than one controlling officer, one for routine work, another for project work. Figure 4 shows the matrix structure (matrix is the cross-directional as well as vertical shape of an organisation) of an organisation that has changed from being a pure line management environment to including management by project. Figures 5 and 6 show the corporate planning process and the project management process that enable the matrix structure in Figure 4 to work.

Change in the way staff are used can create conflict. For example, moving staff from routine work to project work can raise the basic yet vital question of where they are going to sit to do their project work. Their line manager may want them on tap in what they see as their permanent place in the division, while the project manager may insist that the project team be together. With people's loyalties now torn, staff morale may plummet.

Where management by project is already established, we advise you to draw on the experience of others in the organisation and follow the company guidelines, if there are any. Working within the guidelines of a project policy will give you an overall organisational focus. You are part of one big team within which, ideally, you will have access to a **register of projects** and historical information. At any time you would be able to see all the projects in progress and who is involved in them. With this information you and other project leaders and team members may be able to prevent duplication of work or irrelevant work.

Where management by project is new in an organisation's culture, a **project policy** is essential to ensure everyone works within the new guidelines. Guidelines are essential for a new way of working that will suit the new culture.

If you are a project manager or a project team member it is in your own interests to check that **policy guidelines** are in place. They should state the following clearly:

- How projects are to be set up to meet strategic requirements
- How human resource development is going to be handled. You need to know who is going to do personal assessments. If you are still doing an on-line job with its own reporting

Figure 3

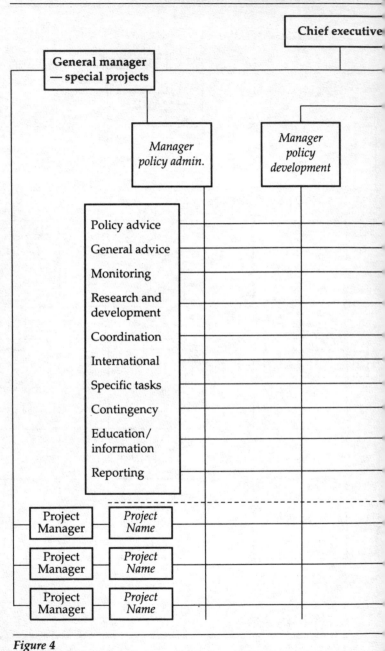

Figure 4

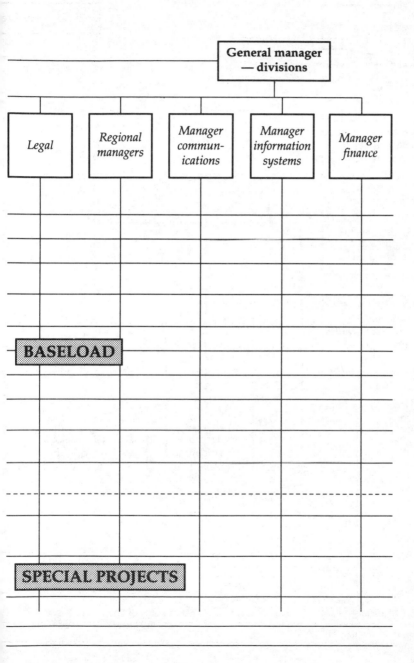

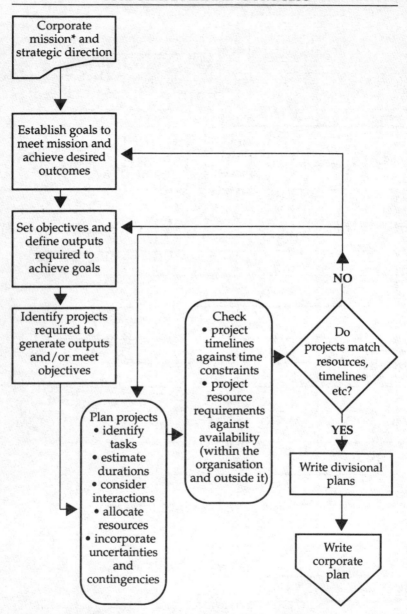

* 'Corporate mission' is a statement of the broad aims of the company.

Figure 5

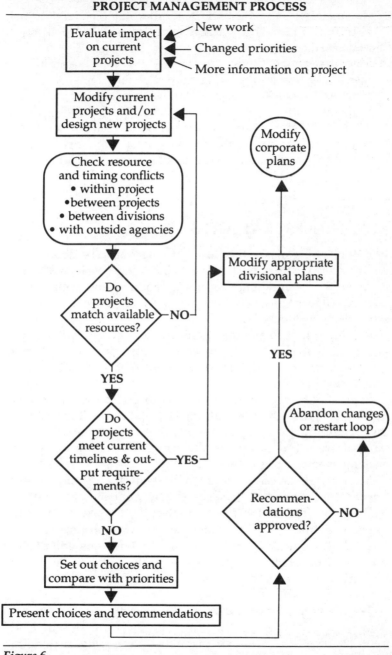

Figure 6

officer, is your career development and advancement within the organisation going to suffer? (You may be spending half your time on projects where you are answerable to a project manager)

- How to negotiate (if you are managing a project) for staff and make provision for replacing staff taken out of line jobs
- How and when to communicate with everyone connected with the project. This includes checking out the terms of reference at the outset so that everyone concerned has the same understanding of the desired outcome of the project
- How to set up the administration of a project register.

PLANNING STRATEGIES

Project planning means thinking out what has to be done and in what order. It starts with the pre-planning phase when you make sure you understand what is required and includes the later detailed planning where tasks are assigned and time is scheduled (see Figure 1).

It is important to ask questions all the way. A result of your questioning may be that the project objectives will change. Whatever happens, the final desired outcome should be clearly stated and approved.

Even if you are under pressure to complete the project quickly, be thorough. Pre-planning is a vital phase. Time taken at the beginning saves considerably more time sorting out a tangled web. So, complete the procedures outlined in the ensuing chapters. You'll never regret it.

Most people in business are well aware that time is money, but if you are new to management by projects, you may not realise how often the two are in conflict. If your brief is to get the job done by the end of the month, and to do it in time will cost more, do you still do it and pay more? That decision will depend on what you established at the beginning of the project when you asked the question. 'What is more important — time or money?'

The following case illustrates the essential nature of pre-planning, and shows how the project manager moves from being told, 'Do it, please', through planning, questioning, negotiating and recommending.

CASE 1 — TAKING TIME TO DRAFT THE BRIEF

Organisation consultant, Stephanie, was brought in from outside to help get a major project under way. When she outlined the start-up procedure, project manager Paul wondered whether the preliminary planning was really necessary. Stephanie insisted it was. She set up a meeting with the project director (the formal representative of the division responsible for the project) for the end of their first day. By that time she planned to have prepared with Paul a draft brief which would be the basis for discussion at the meeting.

The project involved both head office and branches. From the information the project director had given her, Stephanie saw trouble inherent in his decision to use three project managers, a new one for each new phase. 'No one in control will have complete knowledge of what is going on from start to finish,' she told Paul.

After the intensive day's planning and the meeting with the project director, Paul's earlier scepticism was replaced by relief that so many possible hazards had been avoided.

At the meeting they sought:

- Clarification of ambiguous requirements
- Approval for some staff to start straight away
- Approval for meetings to be set up with the quality control panel
- Clarification of the budget
- Clarification of parameters of authority for the project manager
- Revision of the timeframe
- Setting of a priority on time, quality or money.

Paul and Stephanie also included on the agenda the topic of a project manager. They supported their request that one person be involved in the project from start to finish by providing the following options and the evidence to support their preference.

OPTION 1: USE A DIFFERENT PROJECT MANAGER FOR EACH STAGE (the director's option)
Problems:
- The project manager for the beginning would not have commitment for stages 2 and 3
- The project manager taking over would not have an understanding of the project

- Project managers 2 and 3 could blame failure on the work of project manager 1.

OPTION 2: USE PAUL ALL THE WAY THROUGH
Problems:
- Possible biased thinking because of his technical expertise in one area
- The opposition of his controlling officer to his being taken off line duties yet again
- Paul's planned absence on leave at a critical stage of the project.

OPTION 3: USE TWO DIFFERENT PROJECT MANAGERS, ONE FOR EACH STAGE
On analysis, stages 2 and 3 were seen to require the same skills. Stephanie and Paul proposed to bring in project manager 2 from the beginning as Paul's assistant so that he or she could see the project through to its final result.

The project director accepted Stephanie and Paul's recommendation for Option 3.

━━━

Paul saw the light, you might say, about the importance of pre-planning. Giving time and thought to the brief, he helped to ensure not only the smooth running of the project, but its ultimate success.

It's all a question of knowing **how!** The next chapter contains more of what you need to know and do to set up a project.

CHAPTER	*M*ore about
2	setting up
	the project

In this chapter we continue with both general and specific information on setting up a project, including preparing a project brief. The chapter contains details on:

- Four golden rules to apply throughout a project
- The preliminary brief, including the terms of reference in the brief
- Help you may need in the early stages of a complex project.

THE GOLDEN RULES

These four golden rules can be used throughout the project. Their first use is to get clarification of your instructions from the person who gave them.

Golden rule 1 — ask relevant questions

Here are some of the questions you might ask at various stages of the project:

- How clear are my instructions?
- What is the required result?
- Why is it required?
- Is it feasible?

- Who does what?
- What effect is it likely to have?
- When is it to be completed, and why?
- What is my role?
- Who has authority to choose staff and to spend money?
- Do I have authority to choose staff and to spend money?
- How much is the budget?
- What is more important — time or money?

This last question can affect the way the work is handled.

If money is the major factor then more time may be needed to get the job done. If time is the critical factor then it may take more money to complete on time — more people on the job means higher salary cost or overtime payments.

Golden rule 2 — never assume anything: clarify it

Making wrong assumptions wastes time, money and effort. There's no room in the work of the project manager for statements like, 'I thought you meant ...' or 'I thought that was included in the price'.

Golden rule 3 — keep asking about the project's purpose

What you are asked to do and what is needed are sometimes two different things. 'Why?' sorts out the reasons for the project, determines its validity, and sometimes necessitates the consideration of other options. Sometimes this probing leads management to the conclusion that they are requesting something that is unnecessary, or that something else should be done instead. For example, a middle manager directs that an office procedure be changed because all the evidence is that it's not working. Through judicious questioning the project manager reveals that the weakness is not in the procedure but in the training of staff. So keep asking about the project's purpose until you reach the need rather than the want.

Golden rule 4 — identify internal/external effects

If the project
- Affects other people

- Gives rise to additional projects
- Affects other work in the organisation

do the following:

INFORM PEOPLE AFFECTED BY THE PROJECT
Take time to inform people who are affected by the project and formulate a plan that ensures all links and effects are identified. Getting commitment now from those affected will make life easier for everyone concerned.

KEEP THE DECISION-MAKERS INFORMED
Other projects may surface that are outside this project. Make sure the consequences of the project are known to the decision-makers so that timely action can be taken.

Those are the four golden rules. They will help prevent some problems from occurring and will identify and solve existing ones.

THE PRELIMINARY BRIEF

The preliminary brief of which the terms of reference (the objectives) is the first approval step. It usually includes preliminary estimates of resource needs and details of as many of the following as possible:

- Key tasks
- Skills needed for the tasks and staff available
- Priorities
- Timeframes
- Budget
- Communication requirements
- Reporting requirements
- Responsibilities and parameters of authority
- Effects and problems.

The terms of reference

The terms of reference focuses on objectives. It is usually prepared by senior management, but that depends on the level of the project and its importance and complexity. If the project manager receives only verbal instructions, he or she should prepare and write the terms of reference. If you are handed a terms of reference which does not include the names of the project hierarchy, and you need staff to help prepare the brief, then amend the terms of reference and get it signed off with the addition. It must always be signed off, formally approved on paper — a nod is not enough. A sample terms of reference is shown in Figure 7.

Why bother with a brief?

A brief ensures the understanding of requirements and forms the contract between or among the parties concerned. A gap between management understanding and staff understanding may easily occur. The reason for this is that management are there to direct and to ensure results are achieved. They are not the experts in doing the job. Often they do not see the difficulties. The brief is the means by which you, in your role as project manager or project worker, gain clarification of the instructions. You will then most likely go through the process of thinking the instructions through and feeding back information on the likely effect of the action, particularly if you foresee problems. Of course, in the time-honoured way, you will also provide possible solutions!

By making sure you've got it right and taking on responsibility for advising management, you will reduce the possible frustrations of the job and keep everybody happy, including management and the project team. The reward is job satisfaction; the skill, speech communication — the ability to say what you mean clearly, concisely, courteously, completely and correctly.

It's timely here to say that sometimes the freedom to make constructive suggestions to more senior people (the suggestions may sound like criticism) needs to be negotiated. In reflecting on the need for this freedom to question, discuss, even advise, and in negotiating it, keep in mind that it is a fact that sometimes management pass work to subordinates without knowing or understanding the full consequences of the work being requested. Understandably, management's concern is getting results. But seeking clarification and giving regular and honest feedback to one another and upwards are the concern of everyone on the project throughout its duration.

A SAMPLE TERMS OF REFERENCE

DATE: 1 September 1993

PROJECT NAME: Moving to new office premises.

BACKGROUND: As the lease to this building is due to expire within the next twelve months and our business is expanding, a decision has been made to look elsewhere for more suitable premises to lease.

SCOPE AND OBJECTIVES: A project team will be established to facilitate the search for premises through to relocation of staff and equipment.

KEY RESULTS WITHIN MAIN OBJECTIVES (OUTPUTS):
- Needs of each division identified
- Criteria defined for office requirements
- Suitable office space located
- Criteria for lease determined
- Lease signed
- Removal planned
- Removal implemented

CONSTRAINTS:
- Budget — a limit of £50,000 has been set.
- Timeframe — to complete within 9 months. The existing building has to be vacated by 31 May 1994.

PROJECT HIERARCHY:
- Project director — this position is replaced by a quality control panel
- Quality control panel — the members are Chief Executive (Chairperson); four Divisional Managers.
- Project manager — Property Administration Officer

Once appointed the project manager will select a team with relevant skills to meet the project objectives. A project plan and estimate of costs is to be submitted to the quality control panel by 10 September 1993 for approval.

Roles and responsibilities of the project hierarchy are as stated in the organisations policy guidelines. All project members must familiarise themselves with these guidelines.

REPORTS: Progress reports will be submitted monthly and/or at key stages of the project. Report timing and formats are to be agreed with the project manager and panel on approval of the plan.

MEETINGS: Meetings will form part of the plan. Type, timing and attendance will be discussed and agreed on approval of the plan.

AUTHORITY: The quality control panel has authority over the project manager. Delegated responsibility and control will be specified in the project brief on approval of the project plan.

Figure 7

One draft of the brief may be all that is needed, or it may go through a number of stages before final approval. A core team recruited for their specialist knowledge may assist at this time.

THE ROLE OF THE CORE TEAM

Core teams are used where project content is difficult to define. Their job is to develop the brief with the project manager and/or examine the feasibility of the project.

One of the statements that's been taught for years in assertiveness classes is 'I need help'. You can decide right at the beginning of a big project if you want help in setting it up. Or it may be offered. The core team, who may come from within or from outside the organisation, may become members of the project team.

Though it doesn't follow that the members of the core team will become members of the project team, it is desirable to hold on to at least one member of the core team for the full term of the project because of their knowledge of the project from its start-up.

Here is an example of how a core team may be used.

CASE 2 — USING A CORE TEAM

After receiving verbal instruction Simon, the project manager, clarified in writing a basic understanding of what was required as an end result. In the case of this expanding pottery firm (it was adding to its range of pottery, extending its home markets, building up a good export market) the need was to introduce new work processes and modern accounting and stock control procedures. Simon appointed two people from inside, an administrator and a pottery expert, and a management adviser from outside. They defined what had to be done and developed the brief. In this case, both stayed on as part of the project team.

THE ONE-PERSON PROJECT

The procedure for a one-person project is much the same as for the complex project. The brief has to be as crystal clear as for a major project. In the one-person project, however, a simple terms of reference showing objectives, key result areas and critical factors, timeframes and cost, is all that is required, with an indication of any reporting and meeting requirements. The document should show clearly who is involved, their role and their authority. It should be signed off by the person or group the project manager is answerable to.

SUPPORT FROM SENIOR MANAGEMENT

In all projects (one-person or large and complex) visible senior support is essential. Ensure right at the beginning of the project that a senior person is officially taking ownership of the work. You must have someone to appeal to, someone whose seal of approval the project is known to have. It is the person you will go to should you need to gain authority outside your original brief. All projects involve change of some sort. Sometimes the people affected need to see that someone with influence and power understands what is happening. Or perhaps the original plan may change and you will need someone of influence and power who has the authority you may not have to extend resources such as time and money, and sometimes people. Consider the story of Sam.

CASE 3 — WHEN THERE'S NO OFFICIAL SUPPORT FROM THE TOP

Sam devised a training programme that could be used by his own organisation and others.

When he presented the proposal to top management he requested approval to go ahead, and put forward an initial plan which showed research as the first stage. A detailed costing was included. Also submitted were a preliminary proposal for the second stage with a rough estimate of expected key tasks, costs and timeframes — for the meantime only, until Sam had worked out the exact content for the second stage. As far as he went in engaging senior management interest and gaining approval for the project, he did the right thing: preparing his proposal and asking for approval. But as far as he went was not far enough.

Although he got approval for the project and the several hundred thousand dollars he had requested, he did not get official visible support, and he did not request or set up official meetings and approval stages. Senior management trusted Sam. Sam could go it alone, and did, carrying the responsibility alone, sorting out problems and making decisions alone. Of course management were always interested to know how he was getting on, but informally, as it were — a chance word in the corridor, perhaps a chat over a cup of tea.

The initial work changed and grew. The product became one of major importance, with enormous potential within Sam's own organisation. Sam knew it, but although senior management were impressed with Sam's unofficial reports they did not fully realise the implications of what they were told, and as they were not visibly supporting the product or publicly committed to it, Sam found it almost impossible to sell it across the organisation.

Sam's is an example of a one-person project that changed considerably from the approved brief. He produced a product of significant commercial value. Outside organisations bought and used it. His own organisation never got the benefit of it. The staff apparently thought that if senior management weren't promoting it, it wasn't much good. What we said above about getting visible senior approval applies to both one-person and large projects.

Approval by stages

Each phase of your project must be signed off, starting with your terms of reference, and then through the pre-planning phase. For example, additions and changes may occur to the terms of reference.

As you proceed through the detailed planning phase and your needs develop, it may be necessary to go through a number of approval steps before you reach your working brief. The further you take your preliminary plan through without approval, the more risk you run of having to do it again. Take one step and shore it up by having it approved. Think in terms of increments — gradual rather than massive.

If signing off is not the protocol of your organisation, it is still wise to insist on it. Signing off may be irritating to senior personnel, but it is essential.

In the next chapter you will read about the need to check the feasibility of your project at the beginning and if changes occur in the plan.

CHAPTER	**Checking**
3	**feasibility**

This chapter is about feasibility, how and when to check it, beginning in Phase 1 of the project and continuing through all its phases.

WHEN AND HOW YOU CHECK FEASIBILITY

You must check the feasibility of your project right from the beginning. Ask whether it is capable of being done, whether it is possible, practicable and convenient. The pre-planning phase of your project is also a process of checking the project's feasibility, for example when you are identifying what needs to be done and how it impacts on other areas. You are also measuring the feasibility of the project at a later phase as you consider all these factors against the costs and benefits of implementing the project, taking into consideration the criteria set for your project. The feasibility of carrying on with a particular project has always got to be questioned when the plan alters. These are some questions you may ask in order to check the feasibility of the project.

- Should the job be done at all?
- Should it be done now or later?
- Should it be done in conjunction with other things?
- Should something else be done as well as or instead of this?
- Should it be done another way?

Here is a story about a project which is set up to introduce staff training in cost control procedures within an organisation where cost overruns on projects are exceeding 35–50 percent of approved costs. It illustrates how projects can change through checking feasibility.

CASE 4 — CHALLENGING THE BRIEF

After receiving a brief to train staff in cost control methods, project manager Natalie begins by carrying out a training needs analysis. On examining the procedures followed in the existing projects she discovers that:

- Approvals for budget allocations are being granted before detailed knowledge of the work is known
- Project managers approve variations without prior consent to go over budget
- Consultants to whom projects are contracted outside the organisation are not being held accountable for quality results within budgets based on estimates which they themselves have set
- Management have been accepting a situation where the first they get to know of the cost overrun each time is when they are told the final cost and the size of the overrun.

To sum up Natalie's findings, projects are being carried out in an environment:

- Where no control is evident
- Where overruns are seen to be tolerated
- Where no initiative is taken to ensure that overruns in one area are compensated for by cutbacks wherever possible in other areas
- Where consultants are not being held accountable for costs they have estimated.

At this stage Natalie questions her brief. Obviously training is not all that is needed.

Natalie recommends that in addition to the staff training programme she will devise, the brief should now be widened to include changing existing procedures for working with consultants. She notes the need to draw up contracts that place accountability with the consultants, set out clearly when the consultants are to present estimates, and outline the approval process any changes to costs must go through.

Because of the wide thinking Natalie brings to bear on the original request, the organisation now manages its dealings with consultants much more efficiently, and saves vastly on money and other resources that might have been spent or used unnecessarily.

▬▬▬

In checking feasibility, think beyond the requirements in your brief.

TAKING RESPONSIBILITY

The employee in the flattened organisation of today has to take responsibility for ensuring that work being done is relevant, timely and cost-effective. Check the feasibility of your project from those points of view.

Also, it's easy and therefore tempting to work in isolation. But what is going on outside the scope of your own immediate work is relevant. Consider the strategic interaction your project requires, even the direction of your organisation and the effect of your project on the organisation. It may not always be easy to do so, but as we've said before, if you think the project is not feasible in whole or in part and have evidence to support your point of view, tell your superiors — not as a grizzle in the corridor or the tearoom, but present it officially, with facts and figures to back up your argument.

The next case is about a project manager who checks feasibility using Golden Rule 3 in Chapter 2.

▬▬▬▬

CASE 5 — WHAT WE NEED, NOT WHAT WE WANT

The marketing manager tells a staff member that a new production plant is required and that she is to run the project from start to finish, that is from the search for and selection of land through construction, fitout, selection and training of staff, to completion of the first production run.

A project of this dimension certainly requires a feasibility study, and the final question to be asked is, 'Should this plant be built at all?' The project manager began by asking why the new production plant was being built. She was told their oldest product was selling like hotcakes and expansion was necessary to increase output to meet demand. There was no room to expand in the existing building.

The project manager continued to probe. This product, she found out, was in need of research and development if it were to keep up with the times. Expert opinion was that if this were not undertaken, demand would inevitably fall. Eventually agreement was reached that a rethink was necessary on the building of the plant, to allow time for the costly research and development to filter through to the workforce. The marketing manager set up an indepth study of options, backed up by a cost-benefit analysis.

▬▬

USING COST-BENEFIT ANALYSIS TO CHALLENGE FEASIBILITY

If you feel that what you have been asked to do is not the best option, you can use cost-benefit analysis to prove your point (See Figure 8). You may not be a financial whizz yourself, but you don't have to be. If the dollars involved are considerable enough, enlist the help of a financial expert, either one in your organisation or a consultant. If it's not a major project, perhaps you have a friend with whom you can work out a rough estimate. The people who pay the bills always take note of cost figures! Case 6 shows how an appeal based on cost could possibly have prevented an unworkable plan getting to implementation phase.

▬▬▬

CASE 6 — A HOPELESS CASE? NEVER!

Imagine this — a project to integrate the computer and manual systems of four firms that have merged. In each of the four companies staff have their own organisational jargon and their own billing systems (twice-monthly, monthly, quarterly and twice-yearly), and each believes their system is the best one and that the integrated system should go their way!

SIMPLE COST BENEFIT ANALYSIS ON WHETHER TO PURCHASE A CAR

	Capital	Running costs/benefits p.a.	
Purchase	£3,000		
Fixed Costs			
Interest on capital		£300	
Licence		200	
Insurance		200	700
Variable costs			
Petrol		1,500	
Maintenance		750	
Parking		1,500	3,750
Annual operating costs			£4,450
Measurable benefits			
Train fares for two people		4,000	
Bus fares for two people		1,250	5,250
Intangible benefits			
Time saving 100 hours p.a.		500	
Convenience 50 hours p.a.		250	750
(time valued at £5 per hour)			
Annual benefits			£6,000
Annual savings for owning car			£1,550

Therefore purchase car. (Other factors, for example the environment or leaded over unleaded petrol, may be considered.)

Figure 8

Ernie is a computer programmer member of the project team that is to bring about this miracle of integration. He does not believe this project is going to work. He feels he is wasting his time and the company's money. His project manager agrees, but claims management will not listen. There are other frustrations, such as users who last week wanted one thing and today want something else.

Talk to Ernie about this project and he'll probably tell you project management works in theory, not in practice. About the project he's engaged on, he'll tell you you only have to look at the targets. Laughable is how Ernie sees them. So what's the project manager doing? His best, as far as Ernie is concerned. But in Ernie's opinion there's a point somewhere in the hierarchy where senior management doesn't want to know it's not working. Must be, he says, because the project manager has told them often that they need to stop everything and rethink, start again, that the team is caught in an activity trap that is producing only anger, resentment and ulcers.

——

This is a massive project that impacts across the whole merged organisation and involves many staff. It is not achieving its purpose. The people doing the work know this. They are demoralised, have lost their commitment, pull against each other because they no longer feel they have a common goal, sick leave is used as a means of escape from the activity trap and hospitalisation has occurred for stress-induced illness.

At implementation phase this project is no longer feasible. The major flaw appears to be that the project manager is not getting this message through to senior management. It has a chance of working if it is stopped now.

This project may succeed if:

- The project manager can present options to senior management in money terms to reinforce his case when he suggests changes in the plan
- The project manager is someone in very good standing with a proven record of achieving and a good reputation among senior management
- The project manager is someone who can take control
- The project manager ensures that the results they are working towards are achievable

- New commitment is sought from the staff
- A quality control group is set up made up of people from the original four organisations, including people who will be directly affected by the changes
- Ground rules are agreed.

PROBLEM SOLVING AND DECISION MAKING

Problem solving is identifying issues that need attention, setting goals and coming up with suitable courses of action. When establishing the feasibility of a project, problems are easier to solve if a number of people who are committed to the task come together.

All discussion, data gathering and related considerations will focus on the objective. During discussion the following process can be used:

- Identify the problem, its cause and effect
- State alternatives clearly and describe them accurately
- Evaluate the alternatives, separating the needs from the wants
- Make a choice.

The Pareto principle — 80/20 rule

Pareto, an Italian economist, observed an important relationship between cause and effect which can be applied to almost any business enterprise. He believes that it is axiomatic that the majority of the cost of a project is made up by a minority of the components.

There is no need to go into every aspect of every problem. Using this 80/20 rule, identify the highest value items and concentrate on them. They hold the biggest potential for success or failure.

You may wish to measure the benefits and costs of your project against the relevant value criteria defined by Aristotle. If your project is concerned with policy development, these values may be of particular relevance:

- Economic

- Moral
- Aesthetic
- Social
- Political
- Religious
- Judicial.

A good example is mining — it produces vast profits on the one hand; however, in addition to the operating costs of the company, it incurs destruction of the land (economic, aesthetic and moral values), and the noise, dust, traffic, living costs, industrial waste, etc have an additional impact (social, moral, economic values). Cost is not measured in money terms only.

Checking feasibility continues through all phases of your project, especially when changes occur.

The next chapter is all about making the project run smoothly in respect of the people involved in the project.

*P*eople: terminology, processes, problems

This is the chapter where we concentrate on the **who** of the project.

TERMINOLOGY AND ROLES

We picked up early in our information-seeking visits to organisations where management by projects is in operation that a wide range of terminology exists to describe people involved in projects. For example, some multinationals use a project management framework and standard methodology and terminology that is set by the parent company from whom they inherit the whole project procedure. Figure 9 sets out the terms and definitions.

In this book we use terms you are most likely to encounter in business. But remember that the scope of duties and responsibility of any one designation is not the same in every organisation. In your organisation be consistent in your use of terms.

TERMINOLOGY AND ROLE DEFINITION

The name we use	Other names used by organisations	Definition of the role
Project hierarchy	Widely used term	The group name for all the people officially involved in the project
Project director/ steering committee	Output manager	Person or people with the knowledge and authority to make each project work. They 'own' the project, that is, they are responsible for its consequences. The project director (or steering committee) is involved at a strategic rather than tactical or operational level
Quality control panel	Monitoring group/advisory group	Usually an advisory panel formed for the duration of any project which by its size or nature affects a considerable number of people or uses significant resources. The quality control panel may in some organisations perform the function of the steering committee
Project manager	Project leader	The person responsible for the project at a tactical or operational level rather than at strategic level
Project leader	See above	Person who leads a sub-project
Project team	Widely used term	People selected to do the work of the project because of their specialist skills
Core team	Widely used term	People who assist the project manager in Phase One of a complex project. They are usually familiar with the area undergoing change or development

Figure 9

The project hierarchy

The purpose of setting up a hierarchy is to ensure that strategic requirements are considered. For example, if the undertaking affects accounting procedures, the manager of the accounts division will be involved in an advisory role monitoring the work as it affects his or her division and in seeing that communication requirements are met; if it is a head office project affecting branches, a branch representative will monitor what is going on.

In one project hierarchy we were impressed by how well the project team and quality control panel worked when the latter functioned only as an advisory group. It was made up of representatives from divisions where change would occur as a result of the project. This quality control panel ensured that a good flow of communication took place between the project team and those affected by the changes.

The degree of technical knowledge varies too. Where computers are heavily involved (perhaps in installation of a new system), there is a higher number of technical 'providers' as members of project teams. A senior executive in one bank we visited, however, felt strongly that 'technocrats' should be kept away from controlling projects.

The project director

The project director is the formal representative of the division responsible for the project. They usually:

- Set priorities
- Delegate authority
- Monitor performance
- Allocate resources
- Provide guidelines and support
- Act as mentor for inexperienced project managers.

One project director may have several project managers reporting to them; they have higher authority than the project managers and liaise between the project manager, top management and the quality control panel (if there is one). The project director is in at strategic level, not at tactical or operational level, and is usually the delegating authority for major financial expenditure.

The project director supports the project manager by being available with advice and authority which goes beyond the project manager's set authority and work area.

The project manager

The project manager plans, organises and coordinates the work, and leads, supervises, monitors and controls the project. Their role is to manage and control, not get involved in doing the work. It is inadvisable to appoint a project manager who has not had experience as a project team member. However, if it's unavoidable, the project director's role as mentor becomes doubly important.

The project manager is often responsible for choosing the work group and transforming it into a team, and often must engage in the sometimes arduous task of negotiating with senior and middle management for the right people.

Where one major project has a number of sub-projects, project leaders are made responsible for each sub-group and report to the project manager, who has overall responsibility. The introduction of major procedural changes across an organisation requires this kind of structure.

The project manager is also responsible for:

- Providing reports on progress against schedule
- Requesting approval for items exceeding delegated authority
- Anticipating problems and preparing strategies for solving them
- Negotiating for staff with division heads or staff supervisors or project directors
- Showing expenditure against budget
- Liaising at all levels.

In general, projects are usually managed by one of two types of people. The first type of project manager is usually full-time on the job, often a technical expert holding the position because of their specialist knowledge. We believe that the technical expert is not always the best person to deal with all the intricacies of project management, unless they have widened their skills by general management experience. If you are a technical person new to project management, use the technical experience of others rather than allowing yourself to become engrossed in non-managerial tasks.

The second type of project manager is the non-technical person, chosen because they have proven abilities in other areas such as organisation, communication, negotiation or some other skill relevant to the objectives.

Many project managers (as well as some team members) are chosen only because they are the only person available, or because they have time on their hands. Sometimes they are selected simply because they are willing to do the job. Often they are chosen because they have a reputation in the organisation for getting things done. (These people are usually the most overworked.)

If you are involved in selecting the project manager, remember project management is itself a business skill; in particular it is a 'people' skill. Knowing the right questions to ask and how to ask them, and being able to identify and use a wide range of resource people (who may not necessarily belong to the organisation) are far more important skills than, for example, the ability to understand the technical intricacies of a project.

If a project manager lacks an essential skill, but is given the job of managing the project for one of the reasons outlined above, then the cost can be high. Imagine a person in charge who is not capable of establishing good rapport with people, who does not have the communication skills needed to liaise with the project team or other people involved in or affected by the project. It would be a counter-productive appointment that puts the project manager concerned in a stressful situation and undermines the project from the outset.

Uphill battles are sometimes seen as part of the job of project management. Small empires exist within organisations. The choice of project manager may sometimes result from organisational politics. No matter how they come into the position, the project manager often has to negotiate with people in the organisation who have work priorities that differ markedly from those of the project manager. Some staff the project manager may have to negotiate with may feel pulled in different directions through other commitments or on-line work. Others may be in the dark about the project, including managers with staff the project manager wants, or the staff members themselves may be uninformed. (See Chapter 9 for guidelines on negotiating for staff.)

THE PROJECT TEAM ASSEMBLES

Keep the official team membership as small as possible. Small teams work well. A well-functioning team can produce results that far outstrip the potential output of its members. The concept is known as synergy, which means the total is greater than the sum of the parts. Synergistic effect can be physical, in that a group of people together can move an object too large for one person to move. A similar effect may be observed in brainstorming, problem solving and other team activities.

As the project team assembles, and perhaps replaces most of the core team, members will be briefed about the project. (The remaining members of the core team may still be able to serve as advisers from time to time but their contribution to the project may not be seen to be sufficient to warrant appointing them to the project team.)

The aim at this time is:

- To ensure the project team understands the purpose of the project
- To provide an opportunity for the team members to contribute their own ideas
- To gain their commitment.

The project team — time commitment

One of the problems in selecting the team is deciding how much input is required, which determines whether team members are needed part-time or full-time and how long they will be on the project. The problem is especially pertinent at the beginning of the project when it is still hard to clarify how much work the project is going to generate. It is always difficult to judge resource needs at the beginning. One pitfall when negotiating for staff is defining needs too early. 'I require Joe to work on the team for the equivalent of one day a week,' might better become, 'At this stage it looks as though one day a week will be enough, but the exact time we will need Joe for will have to be confirmed

as we gain more detailed knowledge of what is needed.'
Historical data from previous similar projects can be helpful
here. In general, wait until detailed planning is complete before
confirming time requirements.

Problems associated with having people part-time on the
project team are:

- The part-timers sometimes have difficulty in feeling part of
the team
- Their on-line work conflicts with their work on the project,
especially if they are doing their project work in the same
place as their main duties, to which they are more likely to
give the top priority
- Their having two bosses during the project makes it hard for
the project manager to get a commitment since when the
project ends, most likely so does his or her working relationship with the part-timer
- Part-timers are not able to attend all the project meetings and
miss out on the information sharing at meetings. Minutes are
sometimes a poor substitute.

We are of the opinion that part-timers on the project team can
easily be neglected. Also, because they are around infrequently,
they may become slack, which means ultimately that the part-
timer is on the project team in name only. An alternative to
giving part-timers official status on the project team is to request
their participation when necessary as consultants. So, as a project
manager, identify as soon as you can how much time you want
everyone on the team to give, and let them know. If you must
have part-timers, involve them as much as the full-time project
team members when setting up the project. Get them to attend
meetings to ensure they have an understanding and commitment to the undertaking. They should go back to their usual
jobs knowing immediately or as soon as possible when their
input is required. Include them on the information circulation to
ensure they have relevant updates on the project's progress.

Identifying potential for the project team
As project manager you may not have the choice of who is on
the team. Often senior management chooses, sometimes for the
wrong reasons.

If you are able to ask for nominations to be put forward, you'll know who is interested and have a wider choice. Sometimes look outside the nominations for staff who've given up the battle for a change of work. You're possibly missing an untapped source if you assume that the slow in coming forward are all 'deadwood'. Trapped in routine jobs, they may have lost interest in their work and spend their days in a rut of dissatisfaction and boredom. The known names, the proven staff, are usually overworked. Identify skill requirements first, then find the people with those skills. Given the choice of an overworked and possibly stressed person of proven competence, and an underused person who showed a spark of interest in the project when you took the trouble to seek them out, we'd say give the second person a go. It worked in the following example.

CASE 7 — LOOKING FOR HIDDEN TALENTS

Paul would probably have been the last pick of anyone else assembling a project team. But Dave, recruited from staff to manage the installation of a new staff records system in their government department, wondered about Paul. After fifteen years in the same job, dealing with staff records, middle-aged Paul was curt with everyone and becoming more and more negative and cynical about the public service. When the department restructured, Paul was on the redundancy list. Before the axe fell, project manager Dave asked Paul for his opinion on what forms he thought would be necessary in the new system. What did he think about the design of new forms? What sorts of questions did he think staff should be asked in seeking their opinion about the new system? And so on. At first Paul needed prodding — when had his opinion last been sought by anyone in the organisation? But before long Dave knew he had found somebody for his team who not only had experience in staff-related work but possessed a latent bent for administration and coordination. It turned out he also had a flair for form design. The wider implications are that Paul worked as administrator on subsequent projects and was well-regarded by his team mates. The project manager was happy and Paul had a new lease on life.

ADMINISTRATIVE ASSISTANCE

Good administrative support is essential for a large project. The team member taking on the executive assistant role needs skills in organisation and coordination and should be able not only to organise meetings but be competent at taking minutes, seeing that follow-up action is prompt, drafting letters when told their purpose, circulating information to relevant people, keeping project files. This person will be seen as the focal point for communication; as someone with initiative. Their job specification will also include checking invoices and making payments. Figure 10 shows an action sheet for an executive assistant organising a project meeting or conference.

ACTION SHEET FOR EXECUTIVE ASSISTANT
ORGANISING PROJECT MEETINGS OR CONFERENCES

Details of meeting   Type ....
Date to be held .... Start/finish time ....
No. attending ....
(attach list of names, addresses, tel and fax nos.)

Accommodation required   yes/no   Booked: ....
Venue ....
Address ....
Telephone number ....
Contact name ....
Name/no. of meeting room ....
Specific directions required ....

Equipment   Booked:..................
Electronic whiteboard/pens   yes/no
Overhead projector   yes/no
Television/video   yes/no

Catering   *Time Required*   Booked:..................
Morning tea   yes/no
Lunch   yes/no
Afternoon tea   yes/no
Evening meals   yes/no

Agenda   Required   yes/no
Sent out on .... Amended on ....

Reports   Required by (date) ....
Who from .... Received from ....
Checked ....
Further action ....
Sent to attendees on ....

Information (to attendees and their managers)
Meeting/venue details
Catering arranged
Who pays for what
Accommodation arranged/not arranged
Costs
Agenda/reports etc. attached

All bookings confirmed on .... Total cost $ ....

After meeting: Minutes   ☐ written
☐ circulated
☐ amended
☐ follow up action completed

Figure 10

TEAM ANXIETY

Project team members often feel considerable anxiety concerning their roles in the project. Particularly if they are new to management by projects they may feel more visible than in the management system they were used to. They may even feel concern that their careers are on the line. In addition they may feel unsure about how their personal lives will be affected by their time on the project. They need reassurance and support and answers to questions such as:

- What is the team expected to achieve?
- What is my role and the role of other team members?
- How will I do the work? — I've never done anything like this before.
- When am I required — and for how long?
- Where am I expected to work — and who with?
- Who will do my normal work — or am I expected to do it as well as my project work?
- Who am I responsible to? Does my controlling officer know what is happening?
- Who do I see about problems — my controlling officer or the project manager?
- Do I have any authority on this project?
- Who will do my personal assessment?
- Who pays my salary — my division or the project?
- What happens to me when the project is finished?
- How will working on this project benefit me?

It is possible some team members will not ask these questions, but you can be sure they would like the answers.

One person who had recently been a member of a project team spoke about how reassured she was by feedback and other factors. 'You received feedback on how well you had done. You knew what was expected and could focus on the job in hand. The organisation's culture was such that debriefing and encouragement constantly to improve were the norm. I enjoyed being a member of a team, most of all the shared responsibility and support received from one another.' This person is now managing her own project.

One key to team effectiveness is to define milestones and recognise their achievement in a group way.

WHY ARE SOME TEAMS WINNERS?

Some teams are winners because:

- Each individual member believes they can win
- The team and management have faith in the team leader
- They work together towards a common goal
- They know what has to be done
- Their work is planned and coordinated, monitored and controlled
- They anticipate problems
- Instead of saying, 'this can't be done because ...,' they say, 'we will achieve our aims by finding a way around the problem.'
- They never make the same mistake twice
- They listen to one another
- They consider issues that affect others outside their team.

Then there is the team that is neither a team nor a group, because to be either you need a common goal or a common commitment. As one psychologist points out, 'People in an elevator don't usually form a group unless an emergency strikes, thus giving the people a common goal.' Keep in mind those people in the elevator and work on moulding your team into becoming a group that is committed to working together towards the common end, the successful completion of the project. Setting short-term goals is useful here. The completion date in a large project may be too distant an objective for an ongoing sense of achievement.

If there is a falling away in commitment, a slackness that creeps in, with deadlines or meetings missed, or hair-splitting or carping, don't avoid the issue — tell the team that they exist to support one another in getting the job done. Be specific, where possible. And remind the offenders that a little respect for one another goes a long way!

Group behaviour

It was the commonly held opinion of project managers we spoke to that team members will not long tolerate poor performance from a member of the team. The other people in the team are the ones who see to it that the problem is sorted out, particularly if it means they are having to do extra work. The same goes for conformity. Keeping to the rules requires conformity and the team as a whole influences members to conform. Attendance at meetings is an example. One team laid down a ground rule that a member could be absent for two consecutive meetings only for what the team would decide at the time were acceptable reasons. After that they would request removal of that person from the team.

All members of project teams will benefit from informing themselves about how groups start and develop over time, particularly about how the group may influence behaviour of its members and its own functioning. As we point out elsewhere, the project manager wears many hats. The same can be said of subordinates as they give and seek information, brainstorm, suggest, recommend and socialise with the rest of the team.

CONFLICT MANAGEMENT

If everyone knows their job and does it in a spirit of cooperation, why should there be conflict? Because it is potentially endemic in all human relationships. Accepting that this is so makes the conflict easier to resolve. But if people listen to and trust one another and work from a basis of shared information, as suggested in this chapter, and if they are able to give and receive helpful suggestions, they will reasonably expect to resolve conflict. Conflict can exist within individuals or between two or more people. Within organisations conflict can arise within a group or between two or more groups.

Change is one of the factors, and change is always on the cards in project management. These days budgets may be slashed without warning, staff numbers may suddenly be reduced. As well, there may be competition for resources, people may have different objectives, established ideas may be challenged, with renewed conflict when the ideas agreed on are themselves challenged.

Conflict has a positive side. To quote Frank Sligo in his book *Conflict Management:*

> In many situations conflict halts stagnation before it goes too far, and can renew people's interest in areas such as their work.

Conflict provides ways for people to confront their difficulties and work out solutions. Many desirable forms of personal and social change can come about only after conflict. Although painful, conflict is a necessary condition for our growth and development, and a means for us to apply new skills.

Knowing where conflict is likely to occur and specific aspects of handling it constructively are necessary skills for everyone involved in project management.

Commonsense, fair-mindedness and self-discipline, as well as a belief in 'the free and open sharing of information' and win/win situations, are essential to conflict resolution.

Being able to distinguish between personality conflicts and conflicts over issues helps too. In general, it seems likely that dogmatic, authoritarian or low-esteem people are more likely to exhibit conflict behaviour. And some people are honest enough to say they don't like being on teams or committees because they like getting their own way. For such, self-discipline is obviously the way to go when teamwork is unavoidable.

Put-downs are not acceptable in conflict management. 'Why' questions in seeking reasons for someone's behaviour can almost be guaranteed to cause more conflict since they seem to require justification. An already defensive person will quite likely become more defensive. 'What?' and 'How' and 'Tell me about it' will elicit more information and cooperation. Seek to develop assertiveness skills and encourage assertiveness in others.

But first, make sure you know exactly what assertiveness is. It is not aggression, though stepping across the line between the two is easy. If your voice is louder than it needs to be, you've probably stepped over! In *How to Say What You Mean*, written to help people manage difficult situations at work, Norma Michael says you are behaving assertively when you:

- Express your feelings and opinions in a direct, honest and appropriate way, without violating someone else's rights
- Repeat what you want even under stress until you are heard.

Assertiveness makes it possible for you to feel comfortable about:

- Not avoiding the issue
- Not giving in

- Not engaging in unhealthy competition
- Working with others to achieve the best possible solution.

If we were all able to express ourselves with simplicity, clarity and directness, life would be a bed of roses. But things aren't always the way we want them. So, while you cannot insist that other people be assertive, you can facilitate, model and teach assertiveness and assist in a constructive way those without assertiveness skills.

Here are other conflict management approaches:

- State issues specifically, not in generalised or absolute form. For example, you might say, 'You did that yesterday and the day before' rather than 'You're always doing that'
- Get both or all the parties to define and accept the problem objectively without giving opinions. Encourage them to relate facts only, or describe what happens
- Involve everybody in finding a solution and make sure it is acceptable to everyone and that it will work. Consider other solutions
- Listen actively to everyone. Discipline your emotions by using your assertiveness skills to respond (this is almost as difficult as overcoming personal prejudice — also an important factor in communication breakdown). Concentrate on what is being said. Request clarification if you don't understand
- Use a circle set-up for discussion. In a one-to-one situation, move away from a seating arrangement that suggests authority of one over the other
- Take your time.

'GROUPTHINK' AND 'RISKY SHIFT PHENOMENON'

Keep a wary eye out for 'groupthink', both as a project manager or a project team member who may be affected by it. It's another cause of conflict. So is 'risky shift phenomenon'. Irving Janis describes these in *Victims of Groupthink*. 'Groupthink,' he says, 'is a deterioration of mental efficiency, reality testing, and moral judgement that results from ingroup pressures.' Team members succumb to pressures from other, perhaps stronger members to conform and reach consensus. In the process the weaker team members suppress realistic appraisal of alternatives and alternative views. Watergate and the Iran-contra affair can be explained as products of 'groupthink'.

Writing about 'risky shift phenomenon', Janis says that research has shown that groups may make more risky decisions than individual members would on their own. If you are a project manager, perhaps warning your team about these factors will be all the deterrent they need.

NETWORKING

Whether you're managing the project or are a member of the team, don't attempt to go it alone when you know you're out of your depth. Without wanting to state the obvious, we have to remind you what failure does to your confidence. Use the knowledge around you to get the job done — a friend, somebody in your organisation, or an acquaintance. Ask around. Somebody knows. It's called networking.

In Part 1 we have:

- Provided the basic information you need to set up a project
- Provided an overview of techniques, strategies and people involved in a project.

PART 2

PHASE TWO: DETAILED PLANNING AND SCHEDULING

Detailed planning begins

The eight steps that follow provide a basis from which to carry out the detailed planning of a project. Step 1 (identify the tasks) may already have been carried out in the terms of reference. If not, begin with Step 1.

STEP 1 — IDENTIFY THE TASKS

Decide what has to be done. Some projects may have only a few key tasks. In a complex project with many major tasks, the project manager and a core team will make a random list of tasks as they occur to them. Brainstorming (defined in the Glossary) is one way to do this (see *Creative Thinking and Brainstorming* by J. Geoffrey Rawlinson in the reading list at the back of this book).

STEP 2 — PLACE THE TASKS IN LOGICAL ORDER

Sort the haphazard list into logical order. The list contains:

- Tasks that are concerned with the running of the project, that is, its administration

- Tasks that are concerned with the actual work content of the project.

STEP 3 — STUDY THE IMPLICATIONS

Other projects may arise from the tasks identified in one project. Studying the implications of the key tasks early in the detailed phase means additional projects can get under way to dovetail with the timing of the project of which they are a part. Here are some sample questions.

Will the project affect:

- Company policy?
- Accounting or computer processes?
- Projects already being implemented?
- Clients, the public, the environment?
- Staff and industrial relations?

STEP 4 — ESTIMATE RESOURCE REQUIREMENTS

In Phase One you estimated requirements in respect of skills, time, equipment, money. Refine these now in the light of additional information and get them approved. In the following example we pick one resource (people) and look at measuring skill requirements against staff available to work on the project. In a project to improve the distribution of incoming mail in the organisation, you may need only one person with the following skills or background:

- Knowledge of existing procedures within the organisation
- Ability to analyse the needs of the organisation.

A more complex project, say to review existing accounting procedures in the organisation, will also need these skills and as well will require people with:

- Computer literacy
- Accounting experience
- Knowledge of human and resource development, and industrial relations
- Administrative/secretarial experience.

(See Chapter 9 for guidelines on negotiating for staff.)

Case 8 deals with the **timeframe** of a particular project.

CASE 8 — PROMISES, PROMISES!

Branches had lost faith in head office. Head office was notorious in the organisation for making promises that never eventuated, but now, in this finance company, long-awaited computer improvements were under way in the branches. Head office knew that if they were to establish credibility with the branches, they had to perform. Time and quality were the critical factors above cost. All effort was therefore being put into meeting deadlines.

The project manager liaised with the computer people and requested a commitment to the completion time for the new processes. At that time detailed information about the new processes was not yet available. Without it, it was hard to tell how long the work would take. However, when pushed, the computer person gave a completion time that was issued to staff in the branches.

What happens next happens frequently. The full scope of the work becomes apparent and there is no way the timeframe can be met. Management, embarrassed, says the team has committed itself. Management wants the job done because it can't let the branches down. So, quality goes out the window to fulfil an unrealistic timeframe. Branches will have the result on time, but further effort, energy and cost will be needed to put it right.

The delicate head office/branch relationship would not have been further imperilled if, when the timeframes for the computer stage were issued, the word 'draft' had been included in the brief, as well as the words: 'To be confirmed after new processes have been reviewed by the computer division'.

STEP 5 — IDENTIFY THE PROJECT HIERARCHY

The project manager and core team continue with the detailed project planning only when they are satisfied they have sorted out who is officially the project director, the project manager and quality control group. Their functions are detailed in Chapter 4. In some cases these roles will have been established early on, either in terms of reference or the preliminary brief. If not, it would be unwise to proceed with the working brief without them. They relate directly to the next step.

STEP 6 — CLARIFY WHO CAN MAKE WHAT DECISIONS

The levels of authority delegated to the project hierarchy are included in the working brief. It sets out clearly the areas of responsibility for each person.

STEP 7 — MONITORING AND CONTROLLING

In setting up the procedures needed to monitor and control the project you will need to consider what has to be monitored and controlled. For example:

- Cost against budget and cashflow
- Drawings of various authorised staff against budget
- Changes and their effect on the project and the organisation
- Quality of work
- Ability to meet timeframes
- Availability of resources.

You will also have to consider how the project has to be controlled. For example, set out in your working brief:

- Specified channels of communication
- Types and frequency of meetings

- Timing and presentation of official progress reports
- What approvals are needed and by when.

STEP 8 — GROUND RULES

When the team is assembled, inform them of what is expected as a group norm. Here are some questions ground rules would answer.

- Who signs reports — the project manager, the project manager and team, or only the person or people who write them?
- Who attends which types of meetings?
- Will decision making be by consensus, directive or democratic process?
- Who do team members see to resolve personal conflict — the project manager or the person who is normally their controlling officer?
- Who carries out staff personal assessments and how and when are they done? First, check if this is covered in the company project policy guidelines.

Except for the scheduling, which is covered in the next chapter, you have all the information you need to complete your detailed working brief. (See Figure 11 for an example of a detailed working brief.)

Project name: PROJECT MANAGEMENT CONFERENCE 1994

Project number: 0150

Background: Refer to terms of reference issued 10 September 1992. In accordance with the terms of reference for this project a three-person core team looked at the feasibility of running a project management conference in early 1994 with the costs to be covered by sponsorship and registration fees.

Findings: Refer to feasibility report and recommendations dated 12 November 1992 and subsequent approval to proceed to the detailed planning phase.

Project objective: To run a 5-day conference and workshops with the theme title 'Project management for people in organisations'.

Scope of work:
- To contract at least two international speakers
- To present a variety of workshops over the 5 days
- To develop a marketing and sales plan
- To contract a suitable venue
- To set up a communication strategy
- To contract sponsorship
- To ensure costs are recovered
- To implement the seminar.

Project constraints:
- Seminar date — 8–12 February 1994
- Venue must be close to the airport
- Registration fee must not exceed £1,500 per head
- Conference must be self-supporting. A loss situation is unacceptable
- Budget to be repaid by 31 March 1994
- Speaker fees must be approved by the project director.

Project budget: £350,000

Achievements to date:
- Sponsors, venues, and speakers have been identified and approached
- Workshop subjects have been reviewed and approved
- Budget estimates have been submitted and approved
- Full-time release of staff for the project team has been negotiated with their controlling officers with the cost of their time being allocated as a charge to this project
- A detailed work schedule and budget has been prepared and discussed with the team responsible for undertaking the tasks.

The master plan and project cost breakdown is attached for approval.

* This document is drawn up as an example only, and data and calculations do not relate to an actual project.

Figure 11

Project hierarchy:
Director — David Jones
Manager — Bev Reid
Team — Jo Roberts   Executive assistant
     Don Cartwright   Marketing
     Elaine Woking   Sales
     Pauline Harris   Public relations
     John Markham   Training and development
     Gail Evans   Accounts

Quality control — Representative sponsors (3)
       Divisional Directors — Finance
               Operations
               Administration

Reports: Progress reports are to be presented on the first Tuesday of each month by the project manager to the project director. On approval of the reports information is to be passed on to the relevant parties (as set out in the communication plan).

Reports will contain:
- Progress to date and reasons for any differences from original plan
- Envisaged problems and recommended solutions
- Actual costs against estimate and reasons for any deviances
- Recommendations for action outside the project plan.

Meetings: Quality control meetings will be set for the second Tuesday of each month. Agenda and summary of progress report to be circulated to attendees by the Friday prior to the meeting.

Project team meetings: These will be held as often as needed, with a minimum of one per week.

Authority: The quality control panel exist in an advisory capacity and do not have approval authority. The project director and project manager have authority as set out in the project policy guidelines. It is the responsibility of each person concerned with this project to be familiar with the guideline content.

Approvals: The marketing and sales plan must be approved by the project director by 30 April 1993.

Approval to proceed to completion of this project is required after the review on cost versus sales, which is due in by 5 December 1993.

Workshop material must be presented to the quality control panel by 17 January 1994 and approved by the project director no later than 23 January 1994.

Implementation: Project implementation will proceed on approval of this document and the attached plan.

Signed:

Figure 11 continued

PROJECT MASTER PLAN: PROJECT MANAGEMENT CONFERENCE 1994

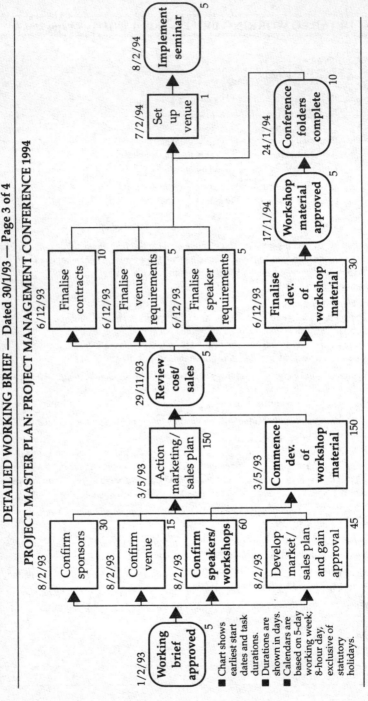

- Chart shows earliest start dates and task durations.
- Durations are shown in days.
- Calendars are based on 5-day working week; 8-hour day, exclusive of statutory holidays.

Figure 11 continued

62

PROJECT TITLE: **PROJECT MANAGEMENT CONFERENCE 1994**
PROJECT NUMBER: **0150**

CATEGORY	COST
VENUE	£100,000
SPEAKERS	10,000
MARKETING/SALES	75,000
DEVELOP MATERIAL	10,000
PRODUCE MATERIAL	5,000
STAFFING	150,000
TOTAL	£35,000

	INCOME
SPONSOR	£100,000
REGISTRATION	200,000
ONGOING SALE OF WORKSHOP PAPERS	5,000
ADVERTISING	45,000
TOTAL	£350,000

CASHFLOW DETAILS TO BE PRESENTED BY 1/2/93

Figure 11 continued

Well begun is half done! By now you know what is involved in the preliminary setting up of a project and how to begin the detailed planning. The next chapter sets out in depth how to schedule tasks and resources.

CHAPTER	Scheduling
6	project tasks and resources

We continue with the detailed planning phase of a project in this chapter, showing how to schedule the work content and resources of a project. We discuss the Gantt chart, a display technique used in some projects, and the critical path method (CPM), a more in-depth method of scheduling using network analysis charts which show the logical sequence and linkage of tasks.

GANTT CHART

Use only Gantt charts for uncomplicated projects. A Gantt chart is a simple display of tasks shown against timeframes. Figure 12, a sample Gantt chart, shows how tasks are listed down the page and dates run across. These can be shown either as daily, weekly, monthly, quarterly or yearly. Also across the page alongside each task is a bar showing the duration of a task from start to finish.

The Gantt chart is easily understood and valuable when a project manager is reporting to management. But its use is restricted because it does not show dependencies.

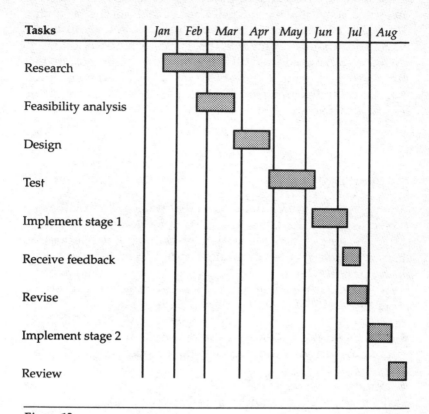

Figure 12

CRITICAL PATH METHOD (CPM)

The purpose of CPM is to produce a critical path. The critical path shows the overall duration of the job. It is the longest path of the project and therefore the shortest time in which the job can be done. It is called the 'critical path' because there is no slack time. Any delay on any task on the critical path will delay the completion date of the project.

CPM is a technique used to analyse the logical constraints and relationships between activities. As well, this method produces, either manually or on the computer, logical diagrams and schedules that show the dependencies and links from the beginning to the end of a project. This visual display allows you to see where you can make changes that will improve the work flow.

CPM can be used to set the logical network of tasks before durations are identified and before resources are known. It can then be amended to show the best possible course with the resources that are available.

DEPENDENCIES

Some people are convinced that all that is needed in planning a project is to list the tasks that have to be done, classify them under headings, assemble staff to do the particular tasks, and then work towards their deadline. Depending on the complexity of the project, this may well lead them into management by crisis, particularly as time passes and they realise their deadline is impossible. What they have not done is:

- Determine the viability of the durations for each task (for example, one day's turnaround for a letter requesting information)
- Determine the dependencies (for example, training has to be done before a new service can be implemented).

Figure 13 shows how one task is dependent on other tasks finishing before it can start. When you look at dependencies you can see in depth the logical sequence in which tasks have to be done.

Figure 14 includes lag time in a logical network of tasks, during which you have the choice of doing other tasks. This example shows the best use of resources.

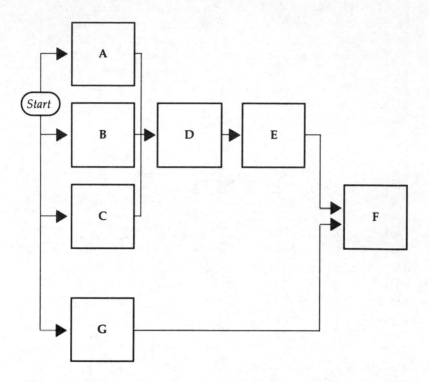

Tasks A, B, C and G have no dependencies. They can start from the beginning. But task D is dependent on tasks A, B and C to finish before it can start. Task E is dependent on task D. Task F is dependent on both E and G to finish before it can start.

Figure 13

NETWORK ANALYSIS CHART SHOWING LAG TIME

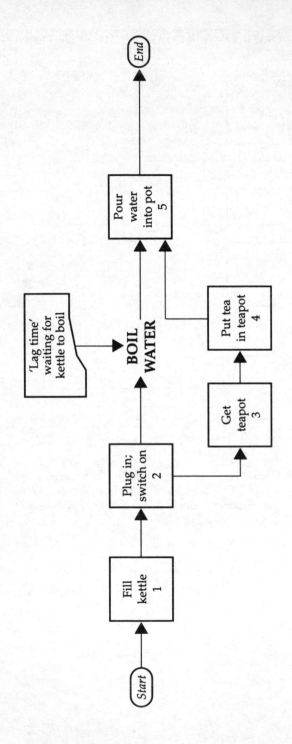

Figure 14

HOW TO DEVELOP YOUR CPM NETWORK

The following is a concise summary of CPM network procedure:

- Identify key tasks, list in logical order and code
- Identify task dependencies, task durations and resources
- Draw your network showing tasks and durations in a logical order
- Identify any lag and slack time
- Calculate the critical path
- Check the logic
- Amend the network, if necessary.

What follows is an example of how the above steps could be used in organising a seminar.

Identify key tasks, list in logical order and code

When you have listed the key tasks, put them in logical order and coded them, your information may look like this:

CODING TASKS FOR CPM NETWORK

Task	Code
Brief team	A
Define venue criteria	B
Develop material	C
Send out for comment	D
Search for venue	E
Draw up contract	F
Prepare speeches	G
Receive feedback	H
Amend material	I
Implement seminar	J

Figure 15

Identify task dependencies, task durations and resources

When you have identified task dependencies, task durations and resources, you have the following information:

IDENTIFYING TASK DEPENDENCIES, TASK DURATIONS AND RESOURCES

Key Task	Dependency	Duration days	Human Resources	Cost Resource
A		1	Project manager	£ 500
B	A	2	Project team	500
C	A	10	Joanna	2,000
D	C	1	Executive assistant	500
E	B	5	Executive assistant	250
F	E	1	Project manager	250
G	H	2	Max	750
H	D	1	Executive assistant	250
I	G	2	Joanna	500
J	I & F	2	Project team	5,000

Figure 16

The lists above show, for example, that task A (briefing the team) can be carried out immediately, whereas task B (defining the venue criteria) is dependent on task A being done first.

COST

Project costs may be identified against each task, or a separate spreadsheet may be drawn up which provides a cost breakdown of the project.

TIMING

If this is the first time for this type of project, you may have no choice but simply to give resource requirements your best guess.

If you ask people who are to do the work to estimate how long they require, you may find that they give optimistic answers. Human nature being what it is, they will probably then try to work within those times rather than prove themselves wrong. This is the view of one experienced project manager we talked to, who added that the quality of the work sometimes suffers as a result. Conversely, he said, a person may subconsciously try to extend the time a job takes if they have estimated a longer duration than necessary.

Where people in an organisation are used on many projects, a master time schedule should be developed which shows the time commitment of all concerned. One person should be responsible for the development and update of the schedule.

A personal project calendar should be drawn up for each person on the team. It shows when that person is to work on the project. In planning their timetable take into account:

- Weekends and public holidays
- Periods when they are on leave
- Whether they are part-time or full-time
  (what does it mean in hours and days?).

Scheduling resources can be time consuming especially with large projects using many people full- and part-time. A computer makes life much easier in this phase.

Display legends on any of the charts you produce so that people who need to use them can see what criteria you have used in your planning (see examples of legends in Figures 17, 19 and 20). In this way you can avoid misunderstandings. For example, in a planning meeting the planners were using charts that had no legends. The charts did not include the essential information that staff were available only part-time for that project, and the planning was based on their working full-time.

Draw your network showing tasks and durations in a logical order

When you have drawn your network, showing tasks and durations in a logical order, your information will look like Figure 17 (page 72.)

Milestones are a part of the planning technique. Make important events such as sign-offs stand out on your schedule. (See Figure 18.)

NETWORK ANALYSIS CHART FOR ORGANISING A SEMINAR, SHOWING CODED TASKS, DEPENDENCIES AND DURATIONS

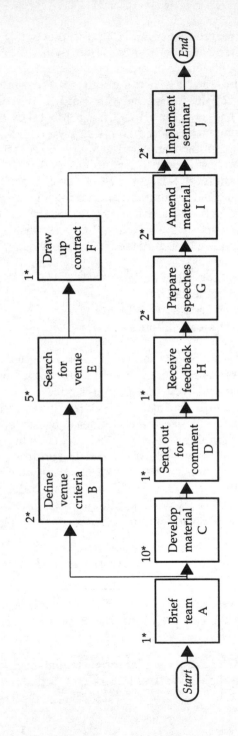

*Durations shown in days

Figure 17

MILESTONES

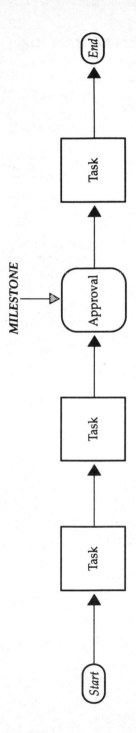

Figure 18

73

Identify any lag time and slack time

Figure 19 identifies time lag between tasks D and H. Slack time is shown next to tasks B, E and F.

A simple way to calculate slack time is by adding up times along each path and deducting the total from the critical path (see Figure 19 again, where the slack time is 11 days, and Figure 20 where the slack time is nine days).

This method works well for simple projects, but projects are usually more complex and their paths not so easily defined. In such projects we can calculate slack time, identify the critical path and calculate the latest start and finish dates for each task. We do this by using the forward and backward pass method shown in Figures 22 and 23 (see pages 79 and 81).

When you draw your network manually, you will find it help-ful to draw your task boxes as in Figure 21 (see page 77).

CPM NETWORK SHOWING TASKS, DEPENDENCIES, DURATIONS, LAG AND SLACK TIME

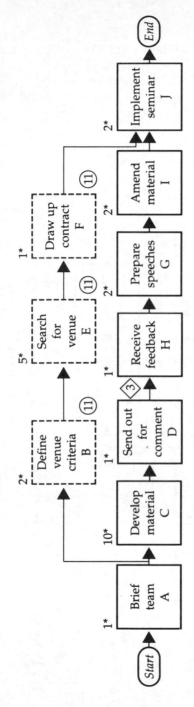

KEY

*Durations shown in days

◯ Denotes slack time (shows a total of 11 days available between tasks B, E, F)

◇ Denotes lag time

⬚ (dashed) Denotes tasks with slack time, that is non-critical path

☐ Denotes tasks without slack time, that is critical path

Project duration is 22 days

Figure 19

75

CPM NETWORK SHOWING CHANGE IN LOGIC AND EFFECT ON TIME

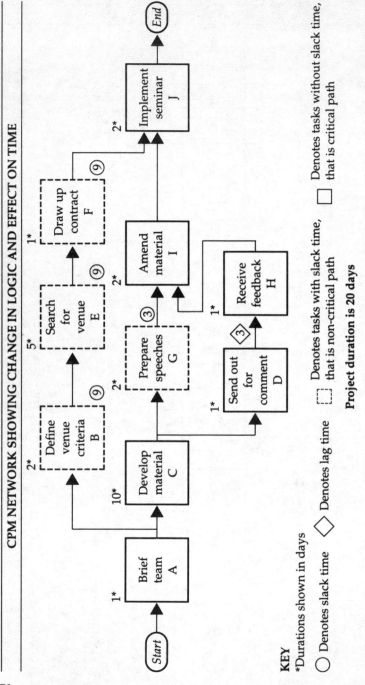

KEY

*Durations shown in days

◯ Denotes slack time   ◇ Denotes lag time

Denotes tasks with slack time, that is non-critical path

Denotes tasks without slack time, that is critical path

Project duration is 20 days

Figure 20

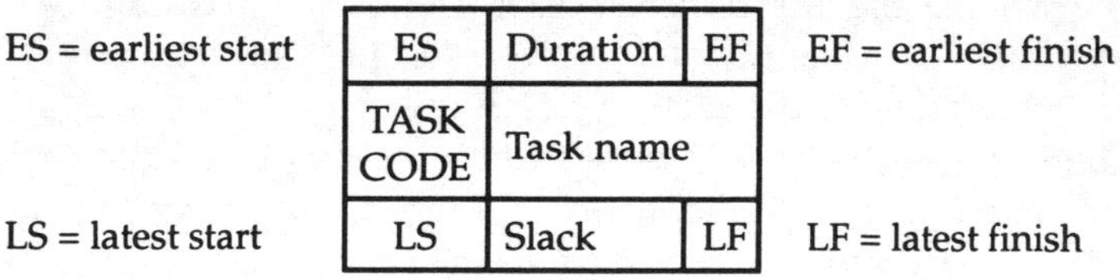

ES = earliest start

ES	Duration	EF
TASK CODE	Task name	
LS	Slack	LF

EF = earliest finish

LS = latest start

LF = latest finish

Figure 21

To do a forward pass follow steps 1-6 using Figure 22 as a guide

1. For first task take the project start date and enter it in the earliest start cell and the latest start cell.
2. Now enter the durations for each task in each duration cell.
3. Add the duration for task A to the earliest start and enter the resultant date in the earliest finish cell.
4. Enter the earliest finish date from the previous task in earliest start cell of the following task. Where there are several previous tasks, as in task E take the latest date.
5. Repeat the calculation for each successive task.
6. Enter the earliest finish date for the last task in the latest finish cell of this task.

CPM NETWORK SHOWING FORWARD PASS

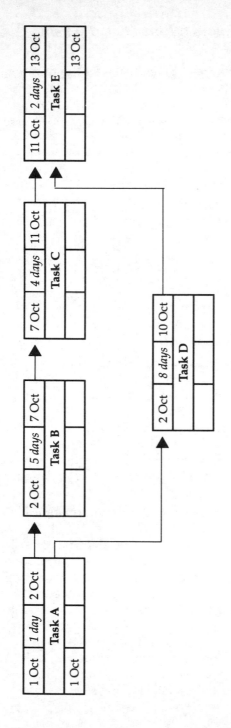

Figure 22

79

To do a backward pass follow steps 1-3 using Figure 23 as a guide

1. Start at the last task (task E) and subtract the duration from the latest finish date of that task. Enter the result in the latest start cell of that task.
2. Enter the latest start date from last task (task E) in the latest finish date of the previous task or tasks (tasks C and D).
3. Repeat steps 1 and 2 for each task, working backwards to task A.

Calculate slack time by deducting the earliest start time from the latest start time or by deducting the earliest finish time from the latest finish time. The critical path is shown where slack time is '0'.

Calculating the critical path

In calculating the critical path we have carried out:

- The forward pass, which determines the earliest times that every activity can start or finish
- The backward pass, which determines the latest times that every activity may start and finish
- The calculation of slack time, which is the time by which an activity can be delayed before other activities are affected.

When we calculate the critical path, the information looks like Figures 19 and 20.

Figure 19 shows two paths with their dependencies. The top path is not critical, that is, it contains slack time. The bottom path is the critical path. There must be at least one critical path through any network. The path must be continuous but it may branch into any number of parallel paths. It is possible for a network to be entirely critical although this is quite unusual.

We calculated the critical path in Figure 19 by adding the duration of each task along each path. For example, tasks A, B, E, F and J totalled 11 days; tasks A, C, D, (plus lag time of three days) and tasks H, G, I and J totalled 22 days.

CPM NETWORK SHOWING BACKWARD PASS

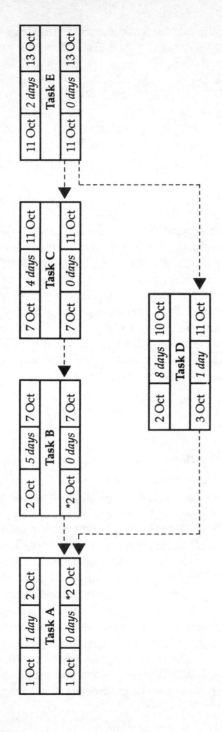

* Where multiple tasks lead back to one task, insert the earlier date.

Figure 23

The critical path is always the longer path, in this case tasks A, C, D, H, G, I, J. The 22 days is the total duration of the project.

When you have calculated the critical path you will have an idea of the expected time it will take to complete the project and will have identified critical areas, for example the tasks that will create delays elsewhere in the project if they are delayed.

The critical path will change as you take into consideration constraints on resources and also if you have to change the logic.

Check the logic

Does your chart take account of constraints and priorities? Once the network is drawn, think about your resource constraints. First, staff. Who is going to do the work? One person? Or a number of people available only at specific times? Time. Are there time constraints for completion of the project or specific aspects of the project? Are there priorities which prevent you from taking the most logical path? You may need to redraw your network to take into account any of the constraints you have identified. Project management computer software will remove the necessity for laborious redrawing by hand of the CPM network.

Amend the network if necessary

We have amended the example network in Figure 19 by reducing the duration of the project from 22 to 20 days, as shown in Figure 20.

We have identified a better way to use our resources! Figure 20 shows that task G can be done at the same time as tasks D and H, whereas Figures 17 and 19 showed task G as being dependent on task H finishing before task G could start. Note the effect on slack time on tasks B, E and F — they were reduced from 11 to nine days.

Depending on the size and complexity of your project, you may decide that some of the tasks warrant becoming sub-projects with their own leaders who will answer to you if you are the project manager. This is where a good computer package will help you to link sub-projects to a master plan.

PROJECT SCHEDULING ASSISTANCE

Planning is usually done by the project manager and people with knowledge from the various work areas in question. However, the actual scheduling, which is a sub-set of planning, can be done either by the project manager or a person who has that particular skill. It is time-consuming, a task that does not suit everyone — the plan is always changing, especially at the beginning. Some people find it very frustrating. Computer buffs, however, with their analytical minds, seem to enjoy the challenge. Computer packages are available for scheduling projects (see Chapter 11).

We have now completed Phase Two, the detailed planning phase of a project. The next steps are to:

- Incorporate the schedule and work procedures in a working brief
- Get the working brief approved.

The project can now proceed to Phase Three, activating the plan. Implementation and monitoring and controlling the project are the subject of the next chapter.

PART 3 | *P*HASE THREE: ACTIVATING THE PLAN

CHAPTER	*I*mplementation
7	and monitoring
	and controlling
	the project

By putting the project plan into operation and monitoring and controlling it, the project hierarchy now ensures that the end results remain feasible and in accord with the terms of reference.

IMPLEMENTATION

The working brief has been approved. Implementation can begin. Remember that although it's been approved, your plan is flexible. It has to be. Change is constant. We can guarantee changes. That's life. For example, implementation may throw up unexpected results which will affect the future path of the project. One of your key people may resign or be taken off the project. Or poor communication on somebody's part may mean that something has to be done all over again. Or somebody in control changes their mind about the direction of the project, project priorities, resources — anything. The unexpected is always lurking around the corner. But who cares? The name of the game is flexibility! You'll adapt your plan. Prepare for the. future by recording variations to projects, setting out the reasons for the changes and their effect on the project.

We'll expand on the theme of unexpected change as follows. You may think you have negotiated a plan with another party or parties, and signed a contract that covers every eventuality. Nothing can go wrong! But consider this horror story:

CASE 9 — THE HOTEL MANAGER MUCKS IT UP

An organisation is being restructured and 'flattened', as Drucker calls it. No one will become redundant, but current jobs will cease to exist and the staff will have to apply for the newly created positions. Extensive arrangements for interviewing applicants at a hotel are brought to implementation stage by means of correspondence, fax and face-to-face negotiation between the project leader (the executive officer in this case), and the hotel manager.

The brief is that by 8.00 a.m. on a Monday six hotel bedrooms, two on each floor, will have been set up as follows: on each floor a waiting room and an interview room. The purpose: to provide up-market facilities in which panels of top executives will begin interviewing the applicant staff at 8.00 a.m. for positions throughout the country, with one hour allowed in which to complete each interview and its write-up.

Co-ordination and timing are critical. It is essential that:

- The interviewing begins and finishes on time
- Refreshments are available on time
- The candidates (who may be under considerable strain — some are applying for a number of jobs), be protected as much as possible from face-to-face encounters with their workmates, against whom they are competing for jobs
- The interviewers (who will be under constant pressure for several days) have their paths made as smooth as possible.

What eventuates is a nightmare for the project manager. Despite the detailed planning and coordination, and the negotiation of an entirely satisfactory contract in which hotel management agree to have the rooms ready for 8.00 a.m., near-shambles ensues.

As it is a race weekend, the hotel is full the night before. The six rooms booked by the organisation will be let out to over-nighters at a cheaper rate on the understanding that the guests will vacate by seven in the morning, allowing time for setting up the interview and waiting rooms. But when the guests renege and stay in bed, the hotel manager says there is nothing they can do about it, and that the organisation should have booked the rooms overnight (not one of his suggestions during negotiation).

The result is that from about 7.30 a.m. onwards there is chaos at reception. Twelve interviewers and four candidates are to arrive for interviews at 8.00 a.m. The happy smile of the project manager who arrives assuming that everything is under control disappears in face of her management who by now are after her blood. From disbelief, through the phase where she threatens to throttle the hotel manager, she passes into control mode, proceeding to sort the shambles out, so that the first interviews begin only fifteen minutes late in the rooms she commandeered: the tearoom, the manager's office and a small lounge off the tearoom.

This problem could have been anticipated and should have been. Remember that golden rule from Chapter 2 — never assume anything! Perhaps the project manager should have negotiated a rate for the rooms for overnight.

Not related to that question, but an important point to be made here, is that the hotel manager was in breach of contract and lost revenue because of reparation. A contract is your protection (see Chapter 10).

Case 10, which follows overleaf, is an example of how major changes such as a reduction in the budget can occur during implementation.

CASE 10 — THE COMMONWEALTH GAMES MUST GO ON!

It could have been disastrous! Their budget is cut after the project has started. And some of the historical data from the previous games is not available, so their accommodation requirements were uncertain. But, in both cases, they manage.

The budget first. Even before the cut, budgeting is difficult. So much is unknown and already some components are over budget. But we're talking total commitment on the part of this team. Nothing can be allowed to adversely affect the Commonwealth Games. So, the frills and glamour will stay. The team brainstorms possibilities and as a result builds rapport with local authorities and interested groups, and comes up with ingenious cost-effective options.

Last-minute accommodation changes are a headache. For one thing there is the cost of the expensive media cabling that has to be dug up and placed elsewhere. It is obvious that at that time the negotiations are crucial between the project manager responsible for erecting the Games village and the person responsible for allocation of quarters.

━━━

The moral? Something to do with battling on regardless! If you're like the Commonwealth Games Project Team, you'll win spectacularly.

MONITORING AND CONTROLLING

Think of monitoring and controlling as an ongoing process during implementation of the project. Monitoring begins with the examining and questioning of the objectives set at the very beginning; it continues through the duration of the project to check progress against the plan, so that timely action (controlling) can be taken where necessary.

In your own project, it will be a matter simply of ensuring that what is being produced is what is needed. By monitoring progress and measuring it against what was expected, you can look at effects and make changes to the plan where necessary.

Some changes you will have no control over, but it is nevertheless important that you not only monitor and control progress but sometimes question the feasibility of continuing the project, or even the need to cancel it. If you've done any debating you'll remember how vital it is that you keep remembering and repeating the premise, the motion that you're supporting or attacking. In managing or working on a project it is just as essential to keep reminding yourself of the required result of the project, or your bit of it. It must constantly be in the front of your mind, just like that premise!

Monitoring and controlling enables you to produce quality results on time and within budget, or take corrective action quickly. Figure 24 shows the need to take action as soon as the plan veers from its plotted course.

By constant reference to the project schedule (see Chapter 6) and progress reports, you assess and control the project.

THE PROJECT MANAGER'S STYLE

We asked a senior project manager with several teams reporting to him what his management style was like. 'Are you looking over their shoulders, asking them questions all the time?' we asked, tongue-in-cheek. Heck, no! He had good staff. He wanted to keep them, not drive them away mad! 'I'm just visible,' he said. 'All the time. Always there if they want me. Always around to pass the time of day.' He called it managing by 'walking around'. But he sits, too, with team members to discuss progress

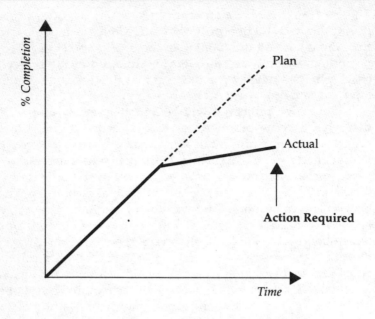

Figure 24

— in their space, not in his office. 'Staff are more comfortable in their work environment,' he said. 'They open up more.' He also said that his aim, and every one of his project workers knew it, was to hear about the problem two seconds after the finder. 'Here's a diagram I draw for them,' he said, and sketched it for us on his electronic whiteboard. We liked it and asked if we could pass it on to you (see Figure 25). You'll see it shows how quickly a problem increases both in its impact on those affected by the project and in the cost of putting it right. The sooner a problem is identified and put right, the less costly it will be.

Realistically, this project manager told us, questions do have to be asked. Sometimes, 'How's it going?' is not enough. Often neither is, 'Is work going to be finished on time?' Being more specific and asking, 'What needs to be done now, and how will you do it?' is at times more appropriate. Know what's happening before the event! You may choose to be a low-profile, non-directive project manager. Whatever your approach, you must be

COST CONTROL GRAPH

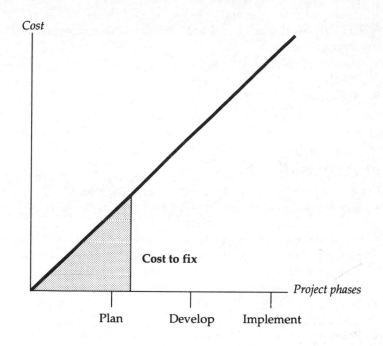

Figure 25

seen to be taking control. People must know you mean business. When slackness creeps in it can spread like a virulent rash.

When you encounter a particularly nasty problem, share the load. Have a brainstorming session to get the problem out in the open quickly, along with options for remedy. Let the owner of the project know as soon as possible but keep the process of damage control under control and low key.

WHAT NEEDS TO BE MONITORED AND CONTROLLED

Here are some specific recommendations. Give them serious thought in respect of your own project.

You will need to monitor and control:

- Cost against budget and cashflow
- Changes to the brief and their effect on the project and the organisation
- Quality of work
- Ability to meet timeframes
- Availability of resources.

CONTROLLING COSTS

The following steps help control the cost of the project.
- Prepare a cost estimate at the beginning of the project and refine it as more detailed planning occurs
- If the estimate is higher than the money available, look at cost-effective options that will still retain quality — an engineering-based technique called value management may help you define the best value for money options
- Include a contingency sum, often about 5–10 percent of the total estimate
- Provide a cost breakdown against key tasks and a cashflow forecast in order to monitor actual costs
- Where extra costs occur during implementation, identify other areas in which to economise.

During implementation you will often be involved in making decisions regarding trade-offs between time quality and cost. When this happens, use your project plan to guide not rule. As we've said, change is often unavoidable. Think seriously before sacrificing quality. Perhaps the timeframe or the budget should be changed. Look for other options first.

You are controlling the project when you monitor progress, evaluate data and take timely, appropriate action.

This process will help things run smoothly:

- Develop a plan and work schedule
- Hold meetings
- Receive and write up progress reports
- Act on information
- Regularly update the plan.

MEETINGS

You'd better learn to love them. They're a big part of your life in project management — team meetings, quality control meetings, coordination meetings, planning meetings, information-sharing meetings. See what we mean?

The purpose of all these meetings can be summed up as follows:

- To monitor progress against the brief and report on implications
- To discuss how the next stage of the work is to be accomplished
- To gain approvals outside the project manager's authority
- To keep people informed and to receive advice
- To coordinate requirements with other work areas.

Here is an example for that last item. The project — moving offices. It can only take place when the builders have completed the building, the phone company has installed the phones and the power company has installed power facilities. Coordination meetings are required to ensure everything is going to plan or to identify any changes to the plans so that you can reschedule resources, and inform all concerned, including the staff waiting to move.

Make meetings work for you. They are a time to build the team into a cohesive unit; a time also to bring related groups together who may be working in isolation from one another. Frequent opportunities to catch up on what's happening is insurance against what has been known to happen on projects — someone on the team, unaware of the change of direction, is off on a tangent of his or her own.

Whenever possible, use a written agenda. Making the purpose for the meeting clear is step one in controlling it. Here are some guidelines to help make your meetings productive.

- Prepare and circulate the agenda and invite additions
- Receive reports for the meeting in advance and circulate copies before the meeting to relevant people (your aim is to provide an opportunity for feedback)
- Set a start and finish time for the meeting and stick to it. One

hour is often sufficient. Try to avoid meetings that go over two hours unless they are planning meetings. Include in the ground rules 'Meetings will start promptly'. You might like to experiment with setting the start time for ten past the hour and the finish time for five to the hour to give people who have other engagements time to get from one to the other and encourage promptness for your own meeting

- Ensure there is a chairperson and a minute-taker.

At the risk of stating the obvious, we'll set out the duties of the chairperson and the minute-taker. The chairperson facilitates the meeting, ensuring the purpose is known, the content is relevant and that the meeting starts and finishes on time. The minute-taker clarifies ambiguities before writing notes, records what action is to be taken and who is to take it. At the end of the meeting the minute-taker ensures people know what action they are responsible for and gains agreement on a date and time for receipt of the results of that action.

Your minute format could include a column on the right-hand side of the minutes that shows who, what, when with regard to action needed. It's a good idea to include in the ground rules how soon after a meeting the minutes are to be distributed. A communication matrix is necessary to ensure reports and minutes are sent to everyone concerned. (See Figure 26.)

It's wise to keep attendance at meetings to a minimum. The experience of people we interviewed indicates that the bigger the attendance the harder it is to control the meeting and get results. If their contribution to the meeting is not really required, people feel they're wasting time.

Project managers we talked to also encourage people at meetings to communicate with others and encourage feedback from people they talk to, contacting the project manager or members of the team with issues of concern. Talking together at meetings or face-to-face rated high as a means of passing on information. Talking provides an immediate opportunity for questions to be asked and answered and for the project manager or management to tune into people's feelings. Barriers that might otherwise arise, don't. People who may be affected by the project appreciate your taking time to understand their side of things, particularly if you show that your plan is flexible, and, if necessary, adaptable to meet their aims.

SAMPLE DOCUMENTATION CIRCULATION MATRIX

DOCUMENTATION			Project manager	Client	Sales	Marketing	Administration	Accounts	Software	Design	DISTRIBUTION LIST
Critical path			X								
Minutes			X								
Time report			X		X	X					
Inspection report			X								
Variation orders			X								
Status report			X	X	X	X	X	X	X	X	

Figure 26

REPORTS

Monitoring and controlling generates reports. Have clearly defined criteria for setting them out, especially where information has to be collated from a number of sources. If there is a set format, information is easily drawn together.

The project manager or project manager and newly assembled team will set out clearly in the ground rules who is to sign (see Step 8 in Chapter 5). If papers are coming in from different members of the team, state clearly if the writers sign individually, or if the project manager incorporates them into one report and signs that (with or without the team members seeing it?).

We recommend that you produce reports at critical stages of the project, but at least once a month. Identify reporting dates at the start-up stage of the project when you are determining the procedure mentioned above. Include the reporting dates in the ground rules.

You and your team will produce efficient and readable reports if you put the five Cs of communication to work for you. Be clear, concise, complete, correct and courteous (and never use a big word where a small one will do!). Show actuals against estimates of work, costs, timeframes and quality. Include deviations from the plan, likely impacts and problems and recommendations for future action. Put the list of names of people to receive reports on the communication matrix.

SETTING UP A COMMUNICATION STRATEGY

Communication is very much a control tool. Watch out for jargon. As a team you'll find it creeps in. Be aware of it and don't use it in your communication outside the team.

In setting communication strategies, we suggest you answer the following questions:

- Who will be working on the project?
- Who will be affected by the project?
- When do we need to communicate?
- How shall we communicate (by report, letter, memorandum, newsletter, questionnaire, video presentation, meetings, overhead transparencies, suggestion box)?
- Who is responsible for passing on what areas of information?
- What channels do we need for feedback and who is responsible for giving, receiving and acting on it?

Getting your message read

Part of setting up your communication strategy is to ensure that what you write and distribute gets read. Do all you can to ensure that the information you send out is seen at first glance to be important enough to read and use. The quality of the format you use, the timeliness of the information and its accuracy, help determine the sort of reception your material gets. To some extent, so does your reputation as a communicator. Keep out of the communication overload business! If your organisation is already overloaded, get through the overload by making your project's material irrestible to the eye.

Make your messages different and attractive, with a distinctive logo, or with a bit of colour coding perhaps such as blue for meetings, pink for action needed, that sort of thing. If it's action you want, make sure your reader knows it immediately.

Help desk

Consider setting up a 'help desk'. One that impressed us was set up as follows. One person in each branch, briefed by the project manager, was the contact person for anyone in the branch with any query about communication to do with the project. The designated person had a direct line to the help desk. The questions were answered immediately or telephoned back that same day. All the questions were logged and a daily sheet of questions and answers was circulated nationally. The main benefits of this were a good flow of points of clarification, and an historical record for future projects.

Having been monitored and controlled through its implementation phase, Phase Three of the project, the project now enters its wind-down phase, Phase Four.

PART 4

PHASE FOUR: THE PROJECT ENDS

Project closedown and the post-project review

THE FINAL PHASE OF YOUR PROJECT

Are you tempted to slump in your chair, heave a deep sigh and forget it? Yes, well, that time is imminent, and you've probably earned the feeling of satisfaction that comes from a job well done. But don't jump the gun! There are the loose ends to be tied up now, the project closedown work that you will have built into your plan of tasks to be done. We set some of them out here.

First, the team will probably disperse at this stage, either going on to other projects or back to their normal roles. Check out arrangements for their next duties before the project closes down. At this time too, make sure you thank your team, and their managers if they have been seconded from line areas. You can do this in the form of a written memo. It's a courtesy which may well be remembered next time you want someone. It also sets a good scene in case you need to undertake any remedial action and want to 'borrow' the resource again.

Make sure that your project files are up to date. The executive assistant usually stays on longer than the rest of the team to clear up the paper work.

The personal assessment reviews have to be done. While your project may be over, it is but a small episode in the team members' careers and proper performance appraisals should be done during wind-down. (The procedure will have been agreed at the beginning of the project.) If you are a team member, you will most likely be assessed by the project manager. In turn, the project manager's performance will probably be assessed by the project director.

The closedown report and the post-project review will also be on your checklist of crucial tasks to be completed as part of the closedown phase of the project. What may not be written down, and what you may be tempted to overlook, is the importance of completing these tasks. We'll explain why they are so important.

If your recording procedures have been working, you now have a history of the project, something you and others can refer to in the future. Based on observations, we believe it takes approximately two years from introducing management by projects to build sufficient knowledge and experience to draw on for current projects. You can now make sure others will benefit from what all of the team learned about what worked and what didn't. The information in your files, in your report and particularly in your review are valuable resource material for others in the future.

THE CLOSEDOWN REPORT AND RELATED MATTERS

On completion of the project work, the final progress report is presented by the project manager to the project director. The report covers the final stage of Phase Three of the project and is similar to normal progress reports. For example it contains information on actual progress during the final stage of Phase Three, cost against estimates, any problems and variation to the plan during the final stage of Phase Three, and effects and recommendations for future action outside the scope of the project.

The closedown report also states that:

- The project has closed down
- No further withdrawals of funds can be made from the accounts
- A fund has been set up from which outstanding amounts can be paid

- Accounts division has been informed of what has to be done and by what date
- All concerned know the official closedown date.

THE POST-PROJECT REVIEW

The post-project review covers the whole project. The person who does the review should not be the project manager, but an unbiased person, perhaps a senior administrative executive. (In one case we know of it was the company secretary.) One company sends out a questionnaire to everyone involved in the project. The answers form the basis of the review. Yes/no questions make the reviewer's job simpler. In any case, you want information in a format that makes it easy to process. In strongly divisionally-orientated organisations, when the post-project review is done by a member of the project hierarchy, there is a temptation to play down any shortcomings which would reflect badly on their own division.

Who should contribute to the review? In a word, everybody. That is, everybody connected with the project, including the people affected by the project.

Review the project in stages (see Figure 27). Relate comments to the scope of the work, project management, timeframes, availability and adequacy of resources, coordination with other projects, teamwork, as well as difficulties such as contracting and purchasing problems.

The purpose of the review is to learn from the project experience. It sets out how the team dealt with the unforeseen, and the outcomes of how they handled the events. Did the team come up with innovative ideas? Record them. Were there good experiences? Record them, as well as the bad. Record anything useful for people setting up similar projects in the future. With the benefit of hindsight, identify what has been learned and include it in the review. The end result of the review is to provide a set of recommendations for the future.

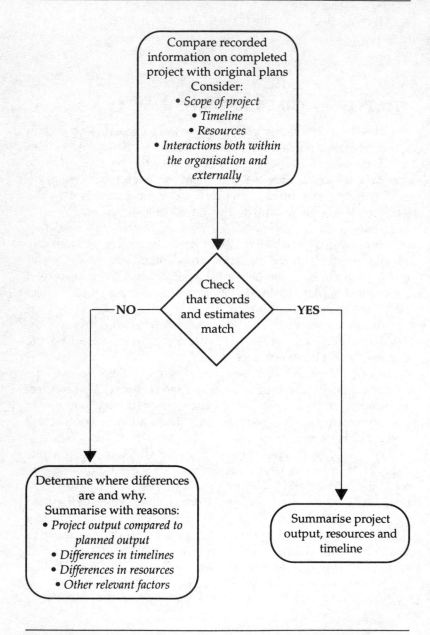

Compare recorded information on completed project with original plans
Consider:
- *Scope of project*
- *Timeline*
- *Resources*
- *Interactions both within the organisation and externally*

Check that records and estimates match

—NO—

—YES—

Determine where differences are and why.
Summarise with reasons:
- *Project output compared to planned output*
- *Differences in timelines*
- *Differences in resources*
- *Other relevant factors*

Summarise project output, resources and timeline

Figure 27

PART 5

NEGOTIATION, CONSULTANTS AND CONTRACTS, COMPUTERS

Negotiation

THE PROJECT MANAGER AS NEGOTIATOR

As project manager you have one title but many hats — mediator, controller, mentor, to name only a few. You are also a negotiator, negotiating contracts with consultants, prices with contractors, briefs with your project director or quality control group, budgets with your project director, and, quite early in your project planning, you may negotiate for staff. Referring to the last item, getting staff in early so that they can have a say in the planning means you're more likely to have a project team committed to getting results.

It is safe to say that every day of your project you will negotiate something. In their book *Getting to Yes* Fisher and Ury say: 'Negotiation is a basic means of getting what you want from others. It is a back and forth communication designed to reach an agreement when you and the other side have some interests that are shared and others that are opposed.'

We believe many people in business see negotiators as people who play games and use gimmicks. We do not believe in negotiation by gimmickry and see no place for tricks and posturing and dependence on a knowledge of body language (Aha! He's scratching his nose. He's uncertain/lying/acting/has an itchy nose!). Instead, know what resources you are entitled to in order to get the job done, be fair, and be sufficiently skilled in communication to protect yourself against the unfair. In project management every project is different, but the basic elements remain the same. The same is true for negotiations — they're all different, yet the same basic elements apply to all.

NEGOTIATING FOR STAFF

When you negotiate for staff you are negotiating for commitment from some or all of the following people, whether they are full-time or part-time. You will negotiate with:

- The project director or project control group to provide staff for the project team
- The supervisor(s) of staff and the staff themselves whose services you will use but who may or may not be part of your team (typists or computer operators, for example). If the supervisors are responsible for allocating the work you require, then it's their commitment you need (see Case 12 on page 113).
- Project team members.

Your aim is to reach an amicable agreement, so no guns at heads! Such an aggressive approach usually means starting from an extreme position and progressing at snail's pace by making insignificant concessions. It is deceptive and time wasting. Save your energy for attacking the problem.

Identify the underlying concerns of the others and state your own interests.

Consider as many realistic objectives and options as possible that will answer your needs and those of everyone concerned. Ask what's in it for both of you.

In the face of stubbornness or someone concerned only with his or her own will, insist on fair standards such as expert opinion, cost, and company culture to determine the outcome.

Working within an organisation you will probably have to negotiate with your project control panel or project director to get the people you want for your project team. Read the following script where the project manager negotiates for staff with the project director, evaluating the project manager's approach as you read. The project is the writing of a computer programme for general use in the organisation. The project is being run by the computer section, but it will need people from other divisions.

CASE 11 — NEGOTIATING FOR A TEAM MEMBER

PROJECT DIRECTOR: You have asked for a team of three, plus yourself as project manager for a five-month period. That's too much. The job has to be completed within four months as we outlined in the brief.

PROJECT MANAGER: I know that's what you said but it's not possible to get the job done satisfactorily in that time. Unless we offer overtime. Is that okay?

PROJECT DIRECTOR: Time is the important factor here, not cost. The job has to be finished, so yes, overtime can be paid. It's up to you to get the commitment of the team. Now you've also asked for Rex, but he will be tied up with another job for the last month of this project. We think you should select somebody else.

PROJECT MANAGER: If the project is to be completed on time even working overtime we really need his skills.

PROJECT DIRECTOR: Well, he's available at the beginning.

PROJECT MANAGER: It's at the beginning that we really need him. The last month will mainly be debugging. Could we have a second programmer to work under Rex's supervision for that period?

PROJECT DIRECTOR: Well, let me think. Yes, okay. We could put our new recruit on to it. It will be good experience for him.

PROJECT MANAGER: Not the new recruit! It'll take more time for Rex to supervise him than it would to do the job himself. It would put the whole thing at risk. *(Pause)* There is one other solution I can think of . . . It may be a bit more expensive but it would ensure that the time limits were met and the standards maintained . . . Chris, who used to work here, is now with the Hastings branch and she could do the whole thing as well as Rex could.

PROJECT DIRECTOR: It would take some negotiating to get her here. What could we offer them? To pay for her time. Supply another person to take over her duties. Then of course there is the knowledge she will take home. Okay, we'll discuss it with her branch manager . . . Have you spoken to her by any chance?

PROJECT MANAGER: Well, yes, I have run the idea past her . . .

———

Negotiating needs planning, knowing what you want, sticking to what you know you can achieve. In the dialogue, was it Chris the project manager wanted for the job all along?

NEGOTIATING RANGE — BE PREPARED!

Begin any negotiation knowing you may not get what you want, though you intend to stick up for yourself for a realistic outcome. Distinguish between what you would like to achieve and what you have to achieve. The gap between is your negotiating range. If you keep in mind what we said about not playing games it will not be a huge gap.

The project manager in the example identified who they wanted, identified alternatives, set a standard they could not go below, negotiated around the most critical factor.

Being a project manager will involve you in a lot of negotiating. Each experience will be different, each team's dynamics will be different. The one thing you will never be is bored. Your personal skills and the use of project management techniques can be developed together.

NEGOTIATING AND CONTRACTING FOR IN-HOUSE SERVICES

Case 12, opposite, shows how successful negotiation results in all parties being satisfied with the outcome.

CASE 12 — WHO KIDNAPPED THE PROJECT TYPIST?

Project manager Kevin obtains approval from his project director to include in his project team a person called Carol, a typist with initiative and drive currently in the typing pool. He negotiates her transfer both with her controlling officer (supervisor) and with her. When he gains approval and promise of commitment from both, he writes two letters, one to the controlling officer and one to Carol.

The letters are similar. The one to Carol is less formal and welcomes her to the team. The main points in both are:

- Name of person concerned
- Description of duties
- Period of assignment
- Performance assessment to be undertaken by project manager at end of period
- Notice to be given by either party if priorities change; renegotiation to take place
- Ground rules relating to Carol; for example, who she reports to and for what (controlling officer for personal matters, project manager for project matters)
- Salary cost to be paid from project budget
- At the end of the project the staff member will return to normal duties or a position of equal status and pay.

The letter to the controlling officer also says that upon a satisfactory performance assessment at the end of the project, a back-dated pay increase will be awarded to Carol.

The project is well under way when the controlling officer's priorities change and he takes Carol back without giving notice to Kevin (not as unlikely an event as you might think).

Once again, Kevin puts on his negotiator's hat and attempts to negotiate a solution satisfactory to both him and Carol's controlling officer. He displays concern for the controlling officer's problems, showing that he recognises the need for a solution; he reinforces the need of the project team for Carol's services; he refers to the written agreement. They renegotiate Carol's services. She stays on the project and temporary help is brought in to cover the other work, with the extra costs paid by the project.

At the end of the project, Carol receives her back-dated pay increase. As well, she is seen to have developed beyond the capabilities of her previous position and is promoted to a full-time position as executive assistant on other projects where she reports only to project managers.

■■■■■

There are several important points from this case:

- What had been agreed had been set out in writing
- A contingency sum in the budget was drawn on to pay the temporary typist
- Carol didn't end up dividing her time between the two jobs. Therefore quality didn't suffer. She was not put under additional stress after the matter was sorted out and the project timeframe was not adversely affected
- Carol was not told about the possibility of a pay increase at the beginning of her project team work. At the time she was pleased to develop her skills and get out of a rut. Had she been told and had not performed well, she would have suffered disappointment. What she got was beyond her expectations and increased her motivation.

In the next chapter we go into what is involved in using consultants as part of the project team. Hints and guidelines are provided for compiling contracts.

CHAPTER 10

Consultants and contracts

BRINGING IN THE EXPERTS

In Chapter 9 you read about negotiating and contracting for staff within your organisation. This chapter is about getting experts in from outside and drawing up contracts for the service or product you want them to provide.

What follows are guidelines on how to identify the right person, how to build up a working relationship, how to decide on what is required and how to negotiate and draw up the contract. Overall, we are talking about being in control of the project even when the team, or part of it, is brought in from outside.

SOMETIMES IT'S CHEAPER TO USE CONSULTANTS

The use of contract staff and consultants is a fact of life now in many flattened organisational structures.

A consultant we spoke to told us of what he called the concentric circle approach of some organisations (see Figure 28). The centre small circle is the hard core of the organisation. The middle circle is the people who come in on contract when needed, the professionals and technical experts. The large outside circle represents the casual employees. It is said to be cost-effective and it protects the organisation from having the wrong person in the job, often someone out of their depth.

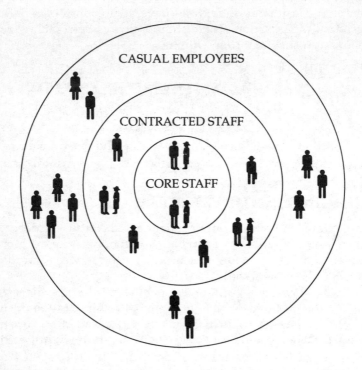

Figure 28

You can get a rough idea of relative costs of having an unsuitable in-house person muddling through if you cost out an employee's time at an average of £15,000–£20,000 per year. Taking non-productive costs into account, this works out at about £20 an hour, and that's before you include the cost of putting things right! When you analyse staff costs in this way and add it to the project costs, you get the feel for the true cost of the work. Weigh that against the probability that the consultant can accomplish more in a shorter time. Also, if you have drawn up an adequate contract for the job, the contractor is accountable for quality results.

Controlling the consultant

Project managers from the private and public sectors shared the view that consultants should not have total control of a project within an organisation. There should always be someone controlling the consultant from within.

Learn from the experience

You can make maximum use of buying in expertise by learning from the consultants. Get to know what they are doing and why. Ask questions. Work with them if you can, and extend your own knowledge.

PREPARING THE CONSULTANT'S BRIEF

We've had experience on both sides of the fence. That is, we've used consultants and been consultants ourselves. On the one hand employing consultants means having to brief and control them; on the other, being a consultant means having to work to someone else's brief. In each experience we've learned that success often depends on the clarity of the brief, or, even more important, on the interpretation of the brief. A simple example: the other day we heard of someone who took an expensive crystal ornament to be engraved for a twenty-first birthday. 'Here are the words to be engraved. Please put them on the bottom of the ornament.' That seemed a clear brief to the person who gave it, and the engraver, who thought he understood what was wanted, began immediately to engrave the words at the bottom of the front of the piece, not on its base, which was what the customer really wanted. Fortunately the giver of the ambiguous message had stayed to watch!

Feedback for clarification is essential. So invite questions when you're briefing a consultant and get as explicit feedback as you can. The completed job is a form of feedback, but if it's wrong, it's too late! Be on the lookout for possible ambiguities and check at various stages that what you need is what you're getting. Beware of jargon.

Let the consultant help you decide what you need

Recently a potential client sent a consultant information on a major national project with a request for help on the project. Budgeting help was what the client said they wanted. At the end of their study of the client's needs the consultant could see that the main area for concern was not the budget, but turning an awesome list of tasks and resources into an integrated plan that could be coordinated and controlled. Of course the budget was of concern. But first and foremost was the concern that if the planning weren't right, the money allocated would be wasted. As well, planning would provide a more accurate idea of budgetary requirements.

A good consultant can help you identify your needs if you are unsure. A good consultant will question you and come up with recommendations which our experience shows are often different from those first envisaged by the client. You may know what you want, but a good consultant will help you identify what you need.

A word of caution: beware of the consultant who may turn a simple request into a major exercise. Be realistic in assessing your own needs and in discussing them with the consultant.

CHOOSING THE CONSULTANT

We asked a number of project managers how they engaged consultants. Most said it was by word of mouth — someone knew someone who had done a similar job elsewhere.

Ask around your own organisation. Phone people in other organisations to ask if they can recommend anyone. Reading articles and advertisements in relevant publications is another way. Also, you can advertise and you can tender.

Whichever means you use to find the person, you will have to work with and will need to build a rapport with him or her. If you don't feel you are going to get on with the person, keep looking!

A consultant is only as good as their last job. So check the person out. Get comments from people who have worked with that consultant.

THE TENDERING PROCESS

Tendering is where a number of consultant firms are placed in a competitive situation where each submits a proposal on how they will handle the work, and how much it will cost.

OPEN TENDER

Where you advertise your requirements, stating a closing date and time by which proposals have to be in. You include a contact name and telephone number for inquiries and send out a copy of the consultant's brief to the inquirer. Open tendering can be time consuming because of the number of people who may respond.

INVITED TENDER

Where you know of a number of consultancies who have the skills and invite them to submit a proposal for the work. This method of tendering is less time consuming and narrows the field for choice.

SAMPLE BRIEF FOR CONSULTANTS

PROJECT TITLE: Accounting Process Review

PROJECT MANAGER: .... (name)

BACKGROUND: The Accounting Division of this organisation is reviewing accounting processes with the need to update existing technology within the division.

SCOPE OF WORK: To develop with the users a computer specification that will satisfy the requirements of the users of accounting data in various formats as specified in appendix X. Also to recommend suitable computer hardware and software; implement the system and transfer relevant skills to the users as specified in appendix X.

Figure 29   *Continued overleaf*

OUTPUTS:
- Computer process developed
- Hardware and software needs analysed
- Criteria identified for type of computer and software needed
- Best option for purchase identified
- System implemented
- User manual developed, tested and amended to suit user needs
- Programme tested
- Programme maintained and amended over one-month period
- Operator skill transferred to users

TIMEFRAME: The computer programme must be running to client and user satisfaction no later than ....
The user manual must be completed to the agreed standard and skill transfer completed by ....

CONSULTANT PROPOSALS:
The proposal is to:
- Demonstrate an understanding of client requirements showing the proposed method of handling the project
- Define who is to do the work: state their experience and enclose CV and referees
- Include costs broken down by outputs. Also details on daily rates per category of consultant and estimate of hours
- State clearly any work seen as necessary outside of the scope mentioned and show estimate of cost
- State duration of validity of rates quoted.

Proposals should be submitted no later than
.... (time and date)
No submissions will be accepted after that time.

Deliver them to .... (name/location)

Queries relating to this project should be directed to the project manager. Notification of decision will be made by
.... (date).

Signed:

Figure 29 continued

BRIEFING THE CONSULTANT

Consultants use the brief you prepare as a basis for drawing up their proposal. Figure 29 provides a sample brief for the consultant. The content of the brief is similar to the project brief. It sets out:

- What has to be done (the scope of the work)
- The standard expected
- Broad timeframes
- The communication channel (who does the consultant talk to and who not — this needs to be handled carefully to keep control)
- Progress reporting, which should preferably be a written weekly or monthly report under headings such as:
  - progress against objectives for last reporting period
  - problems experienced
  - resolution plans
  - resource position
  - objectives for next reporting period
  - brief comment on project status versus plan. This reporting is valuable as both a project monitoring tool and as a basis for tracking the performance of the consultant. It basically keeps the consultant honest
- Knowledge transfer, which ensures that knowledge is transferred from the consultant to the people in your organisation in the areas vital to the ongoing support of whatever it is the consultant is helping you with. It involves statements along the lines of 'By the completion of the contract task, our own people will have the knowledge to . . .'

The brief asks for proposals which detail:

- How the consultant/s will handle the work
- How much it will cost (does the cost include VAT?)
- Who will do the work, and their curricula vitae
- Names of referees.

One experienced project manager said, 'I have seen many tender evaluations end up in chaos and taking forever because a response format was not included in the request. What you need is a list of headings and specific questions to be answered in the tender response. Also, make sure any special industrial issues arising from non-company staff working on-site are covered (for example, your organisation might be smoke-free, etc).'

The brief for the consultant is so important you may wish to use a consultant to help you prepare it, unless it's a straightforward brief you can handle, or you are an expert in the area in which the consultant is going to work. Specific language ensures that a number of consultants will interpret the brief the same way — otherwise you'll be comparing apples with oranges! The consultant who draws up the brief should be paid even if the contract does not eventuate. This applies to one brought in to prepare the brief or to one who is also tendering for the job.

Inviting the consultants in for a briefing

Usually copies of a project brief are sent out, but bringing a group of tendering consultants in for a briefing session saves time. It also gives the consultants an opportunity to discuss issues and clarify specific areas which may be unclear.

An organisation we visited was engaged in the management of a change that was affecting employees throughout the country. They sent out an overview of their requirements to 20 consultancy firms, inviting each one to submit a proposal. Some firms declined, but 15 replied. Out of the 15, seven were shortlisted. The shortlisted firms were invited to an open briefing session. The project manager prepared a short presentation and then invited questions from the audience.

The feedback from the consultants was that they found it beneficial to be able to clarify a number of issues. Two firms dropped out at this stage and the other five were asked to come back at different times within a week and make a presentation to the project control group and project team. Each firm was allowed fifteen minutes to present their proposal. Refreshments at the end of their presentations enabled the consultants and project team to mix and get to know each other and to answer the question, 'Can we work with these people?'

At each stage of this procedure the consultants were measured against careful predetermined criteria (see 'Analysing proposals' on the following page).

This type of briefing session is used where the requirements are complex and costs are high.

PROPOSALS

Where it is possible, request that prices quoted on a proposal be itemised against the key tasks. This makes it easier for costing purposes, especially if part of the work is deducted at a later stage.

It sometimes happens that an organisation takes a long time to decide on which proposal to accept. This can affect the costs originally quoted. Ask that the period for which the price is valid be stated in the proposal.

ANALYSING PROPOSALS

You have received proposals which are easy to analyse because of the format you requested in your brief. You may be tempted to go straight to the bottom line, as they say. But remember price isn't everything. Value for money and the ability of the firm to give you what you need is important. Often people take the lowest price without giving enough thought to other criteria and end up paying more in the long run.

The important thing to remember is to keep your options open until you are sure that you have got the right person for the job. You may need to talk to some of the applicant consultants. Bringing them in and talking to them doesn't mean they have a contract.

As a result of your analysis of the proposals you may decide to employ more than one firm to do the work, dovetailing the weakness of one firm with the strength of another to give you optimum performance. Or the need for haste may dictate your need for more than one consultant.

Procedure for analysing the proposal

Measure the suitability of the consultant against set criteria for performing the project tasks. The information from the analysis also provides you with the means to respond to requests that may be made under the Official Information Act concerning your selection method.

Follow this two-step procedure:

Step 1

Identify criteria for measuring suitability, for example:

- Price
- Time
- Staff available
- Guarantees

- Presentation
- References
- Demonstrated experience.

Step 2

Draw up a matrix showing the firms across the top and the criteria down the side.

In the example in Figure 30 we have four proposers whom we have coded A, B, C and D. Each of them has been ranked one to four against each of the criteria, with four being the most desirable. The score for each criterion for each proposer was then weighted by multiplying by the figure given in the weighting column. (The weighting factor is an arbitrary figure decided by the degree of importance placed on the criteria by the project team.)

EXAMPLE OF AN EVALUATION MATRIX REPRESENTING FOUR PROPOSALS

Critical factors	Weighting	PROPOSERS			
		A	B	C	D
Price	3	1 (3)	3 (9)	2 (6)	4 (12)
Experience	4	2 (8)	1 (4)	4 (16)	3 (12)
Time	3	4 (12)	2 (6)	3 (9)	1 (3)
Staff	4	2 (8)	1 (4)	4 (16)	3 (12)
Guarantee	2	3 (6)	4 (8)	2 (4)	1 (2)
Presentation	3	4 (12)	3 (9)	2 (6)	1 (3)
References	3	1 (3)	3 (9)	2 (6)	4 (12)
Totals		52	49	63	56

Figure 30

The example in Figure 30 shows that the proposal from Company C has the best score.

Be guided to some extent by your gut feeling about the consultants concerned, regardless of whether they have the top score. Once you've made your decision you are ready to negotiate a contract with the firm in question. A sample of a proposal evaluation sheet that was used for a management of change project is shown in Figure 31.

SAMPLE PROPOSAL EVALUATION FOR MANAGEMENT OF CHANGE PROJECT

CRITERIA		Structures	Processes	Performance	HO/BR Interaction	Management of Change	TOTALS
Experience	► H						
References	► H						
Availability	► H						
Skill transfer		M	H	M	M	M	
Accountability	► H						
Scope of adequacy	► H						
Act jointly	► M						
Price	► M						
Location	► L						
TOTALS							

Score 1-10
High X[3]   Medium X[2]   Low X[1]

Figure 31

THE CONTRACT

The contract is a flexible working document with monitoring and control mechanisms built into it. It is important in a dispute. Its main value, however, lies in the process of setting it up, during which the parties concerned clarify issues and come up with a scope of work, ground rules, guidelines and costs which are agreed to and understood by both or more parties.

125

Different ways of pricing a contract

FIXED PRICE

Where all the risk is with the contractor as far as cost is concerned. There can be no claims for extra costs unless the client issues a request for variation to the contract and the cost of the variation is agreed as an extra to the contract price.

Fixed price contracts are advisable where the content of the work is known and the duration of the contract is for a maximum of twelve months. The fixed price takes into account estimated increases in cost over the period of the contract. Entering into a fixed price contract for longer than a twelve-month period is unwise; unrealistic estimates of price fluctuations can be built into the price. You may be paying a high premium for the risk the consultant is taking.

When a consultant agrees a fixed price, they are agreeing to the contents of the brief as being accurate and comprehensive. If during the contract, work not specified is necessary to finish the job, it cannot be charged as an extra. You will have to be careful here and decide on what is fair. Sometimes genuine mistakes are made and a negotiated agreement needs to be reached to keep good faith on both sides. Too often though, consultants tendering for work, put in a low price knowing that the scope of work has holes in it and that they can make their money on variations to the contract.

A fixed price contract is the most frequently used in organisations.

ESCALATING PRICE

Where a price is agreed at today's rates, with an agreement to pay for market price escalations over the duration of the contract. This type of contract is commonly used for projects spanning more than twelve months. You might use such a contract on a project to build a new office or to refurbish and fit out an existing office. Be careful of this contract if you are weak on control. There is an incentive for the contractor not to begin or complete on time — the later they are the higher their claims for increased costs. No increased costs should be payable for work done after the due completion date unless variation orders issued by you have increased the time required to do the job. Put it in your contract.

HOURLY RATE

Where you're contracting for smaller jobs, especially where the work content is unknown. There's an obvious drawback — the contract is based on trust and there may be an incentive for the contractor to take longer to complete. Also, with your budget in mind, you'd like to know your all-up costs in advance. You can, of course, place a maximum number of hours on the work and specify a time well in advance at which you are to be notified if overruns are foreseen.

PERCENTAGE FEES

Where a percentage of the final contract price is paid to the consultant. We don't like this one. It penalises the effective contractor who works hard to control costs, and lines the pockets of the not-so-effective. For example, under the terms of contract where the consultant is to receive 10 percent of the final cost of the project, there is no incentive to control costs.

CONTRACT PAYMENTS

Where you pay a lump sum or pay progress payments.

RETENTION OF PERCENTAGE OF THE PRICE

Where, in some contracts, it is beneficial when making payment arrangements to hold at least 20 percent of the price for payment on completion, as protection against failure to meet time or quality objectives.

HIDDEN COSTS

Where, for example, a cost of £500 a day may be shown plus expenses. You may find too late that your consultant's expenses include flying home to Tauranga from Wellington each weekend, or staying in the top hotel. Specify limits of expenditure on particular items. Also some consultancies try to charge extra for secretarial and photocopying services, or even add 5 percent to invoices for processing them.

ESTIMATES

Where the organisation prepares a cost estimate before requesting proposals, preferably using historical information from previous similar jobs.

Contract checklist

The contract should cover:

- The scope of the work
- The client hierarchy
- The consultant hierarchy
- Reporting requirements
- The approval process
- Price breakdown
- The type of contract pricing
- The process for handling variations to the contract
- Payment: when payment will be made, and the method of payment
- Timeframes — start and finish dates and major time commitments within the contract
- Penalties for late completion
- Escape clauses for early termination of the contract
- Substitution of consultant
- Confidentiality of your organisation's information during and after the contract.

Figure 32 provides an example of a contract for employing consultants.

Notes of caution

STANDARD CONTRACTS OFFERED BY CONSULTANTS

Look at these contracts very carefully. They will generally be biased in favour of the consultant and are the consultant's first position in negotiating a deal. Don't necessarily accept the line, 'This is our standard contract and you must sign it.' The customer is always right. You are paying for the service. The terms should match your need, not the consultant's. For example, if your work hours are 8.00 a.m. – 4.30 p.m. and the consultant has his contract hours as 9.00 a.m. to 6.00 p.m., it can be frustrating in getting a team approach working for *you*. Delete or amend relevant clauses as agreed, or write a covering letter with your requirements which becomes part of the contract.

Be careful here. In discussion with the consultants you may be led to suppose you are getting their best person.

It is important that the contract specifies who is doing the work and that you are satisfied you are getting the experience you are paying for. Stipulate in the contract that a replacement, if one is necessary, will be a person of equal seniority and good standing.

SAMPLE OF A CONTRACT FOR EMPLOYING CONSULTANTS

PROJECT TITLE: Accounting Process Review

This Contract is between .... (the employer)
and

.... (the contractor)

It is a *Fixed* price contract for the sum of $ ....
.... Dollars
(the contract sum includes VAT)

SCOPE OF WORK: As detailed in consultant proposal and amendments
dated .... The proposal as amended forms part of this
contract as Appendix 1.

TIMEFRAME:
Work to commence on ....
Stage one to be completed by ....
Final stage completed by ....
Time is of the essence in this contract and a penalty of £.................... per
day is payable by the contractor to the employer for overruns in time
due to contractor negligence.

CLIENT HIERARCHY:
Project manager ....
Project team ....
Project director ....

Figure 32

CONSULTING HIERARCHY:
Senior consultant ....
Programmer ....

SUBSTITUTIONS: No substitution of consultants will be made without the approval of the project manager. Any such substitutions will take into account experience and seniority required for the position. A replacement must be of equal standing.

REPORTING: The senior consultant reports to the project manager. Directions for the project are conveyed through the project manager to the senior consultant.

Progress reports are expected on the 20th of each month and at critical stages. Dates for submission and expected format to be agreed with the consultant and project manager.

CONTRACT VARIATION PROCEDURE:
- No variation is to be issued without approval of the project manager.
- The variation is to show whether it is extra work or a reduction in work content; any expected cost increase or reduction; other effects such as time extensions and delays, especially where this affects other areas of the project.

APPROVAL PROCESS: All approvals will be made by the project manager or where necessary be put forward to the project director.

PAYMENT:
- Progress payments will be made on completion of each phase of the project within .... (days) of receipt of approved invoice.
- Twenty percent of the contract price will be retained until satisfactory completion of the maintenance period.

Either party retains the right to terminate this contract upon receipt by the other of written notification of termination giving a minimum of seven days' notice. Costs incurred up to termination must be paid.

Figure 32 continued

CASE 13 — SWITCH THE CONSULTANT

In one public project (we regret we cannot reveal our sources) a senior consultant was taken off the job and replaced by a junior who had to be supervised. This person could not report directly to the client. Delays and frustrations built up as a result of his having to report to his senior consultant who then reported to the client. It wasn't good enough! The project manager took control and insisted on the appropriate measures being taken — the reinstatement of the senior consultant or someone of equal seniority. There was no problem — it was all in the contract!

Take the precaution of finding out how heavily committed your consultant is. Can you get the person you want? Can they deliver?

Escape clauses

Your needs may change. You may regret choosing that particular consultant. Sometimes what you have contracted for is not working.

We spoke to one project manager who was trying radio advertising for the first time. It's not cheap. If it didn't work, thousands of dollars would be wasted. The sales consultant was fair and reasonable. They negotiated an agreement with something in it for both of them: payment in advance of the usual date, and a cut-off point for the user if the advertising wasn't working (that is, if fewer than a given number of calls were received in a given time in response to the advertisement).

Contract variations

Where changes to initial requirements are necessary or where contract documentation proves inadequate. The process for handling variations is part of your contract. Agree the price for the extra work before the work is undertaken. If the extra work negates other work included in the contract price, the cost of the work being excluded is deducted from the contract price.

Time is a major factor in contract variations. Will a variation increase, reduce or not affect the timing? In view of the penalty clause for late completion, should you set a new completion date? Establish effects on other areas of the project outside this contract.

Case 14, which follows, illustrates the importance of having a contract.

CASE 14 — THE CONTRACT SAVES THE DAY

The contract was for the purchase of computer software and programming a database. When the product was delivered, it was not as contracted for. The retailer maintained that what was ordered was not feasible. What they provided was a locked-off product into which only they could put amendments in the future, at considerable, ongoing cost to the purchaser.

The representative of the purchasing organisation knew that a package was available which would allow the organisation to make changes in the future, and that was what they had contracted for with the retailer. The purchasing organisation informed the retailer that they were considered in breach of contract and that they would not be paid if the software as contracted for were not delivered within a certain time. The retailer delivered.

In Case 15 we see the risk inherent in not having control mechanisms set out in the contract.

CASE 15 — LET'S BUILD A CONSERVATORY

Stella and Bill used the contractor's basic contract. Much of what was discussed and agreed upon did not go in the contract. It was that sort of relationship, based largely on trust and a 'let the subcontractor Joe get on with the job' attitude. The contractor promised completion for November with a contract period of three weeks.

The project began to fall behind schedule. The quality of work was well below standard. Work stopped. Numerous phone calls to the contractor made no difference. February came, and still nothing had been done to rectify the situation. Twenty major defects had been identified, including serious leakage into the conservatory.

At this late date Stella and Bill took control. Their letter to the contractor stated that he was in breach of contract, that unless he met with them within the next seven days and began work that the contract would be considered null and void and no further payment would be made. They stated their intention to bring in another contractor. The contractor agreed that he was in breach of contract. He was a tradesperson new at managing. He couldn't cope. Both parties lost — the contractor because he didn't get paid, and Stella and Bill because though they now have a conservatory that has been put right as far as possible, they have to live with some of the irreversible faults.

You can learn a couple of things here. One is that you have little or no control over sub-contractors. But the major concern is the failure to agree on control procedures with the main contractor. Stella and Bill could have set it in place early: weekly meetings with the contractor, a signed contract saying specific stages would be signed off on completion on a certain date and payment made at each stage. The contractor would have seen from the beginning that these clients meant business and that if any job would suffer it wouldn't be that one.

KEEPING CONTROL AND MAINTAINING CONSULTANT ACCOUNTABILITY

The consultant may be an expert in their field, but you are the best interpreter of how useful that expertise is to you.

If you are dealing with consultants for the first time, get over your politeness and timidity. There's no need to be confrontational or aggressive, but you do want to stay in the driver's seat. Control and confidence go together.

You're in control when you request clarification, when you insist on terminology you understand, when you keep the consultant working to your agenda, not theirs. (A good sales-person will not seek to supply you with inappropriate products but even the best will tend to analyse your needs in terms of what they sell.)

You're in control when you insist reports come in on time, when you read, discuss and question them where necessary.

If you keep changing your mind as to what is required and alter or ignore a consultant's recommendation, you are reducing if not nullifying their accountability. Do not change the consultant's recommendations. If you think the consultant is wrong, talk about it. If the consultant stands by the recommendations, add your own comments as a separate paper. The consultant may be wrong, but their accountability must be maintained. A consultant cannot be held responsible if their work has been changed.

In this chapter we have highlighted what we feel are the main points to keep in mind in engaging contracted staff. Remember your aim must always be value for money.

*M*aking best use of the computer

THE COMPUTER IS AS GOOD AS . . .

A computer is a tool, no more than that. It has no magical properties; it will not do the work for you, and if misused will give you wrong information back. But if you first master the principles of project management, and understand the manual process of calculating project schedules before you attempt to rely on computer technology, a good project management software package will help you to manage your project and save you many hours in the process.

Be realistic about the computer. It gives you the same information as if you did the work manually. It is going to take you as long to put the initial information into the computer as it would take you to record it manually. There are no short-cuts there. But (and it's a big 'but'), you will save many hours from then on, especially if there are changes, and there usually are many! Used properly, your computer will reward you in a number of ways. It can speedily select and display data that you can use to plan, monitor, control and amend the project. Reports can also be generated in a number of formats.

NETWORK ANALYSIS CHART

The computer will allow you to manipulate data and give you instant feedback on the effects of your changes. (For details of the network analysis chart, see Chapter 6.)

GANTT CHART

From the information that has gone into the network analysis chart, you can produce the Gantt chart or any specific piece of information that you want from the Gantt chart. For example you can request that it display all the tasks or just critical tasks.

LIST OF RESOURCES CHART

You can request, for example, a list of people working on the project.

PROJECT TABLE

This will give you information on tasks: start and finish times; slack times; estimated durations; estimated cost; progress against estimates. The amount of information displayed can be altered to suit your own reporting requirements.

CHOOSING THE RIGHT PROJECT MANAGEMENT PACKAGE

You have many to choose from. We have graded software into three ranges according to cost: low, medium and high. The low to medium price range should meet most organisational project needs. The higher price range is usually for complex construction projects and may be too technical for your needs. In fact, 'too technical for our needs' was a comment we heard several times from project team members about their expensive computer software. So give thought to your needs. For example, on a one-person project you may be interested only in scheduling tasks. Or scheduling resources may be a major requirement. Budget and cashflow information is often not required; it's usually easier to use a single spreadsheet.

In choosing the software, consider who will be using it. Is it a one-off for yourself or will it be used by people across the organisation? What are the needs of the users? Will it be used on micro or networked on the main computer system?

If the package is for the organisation, ask the users what their needs are. Often they don't know, so here are a few points you can cover:

- Ease of data entry and amendments
- Good visual display
- Choice of charts and report formats
- Something easy to learn and use
- Training
- Back-up service from supplier
- Task scheduling
- Resource scheduling
- Multiple calendars
- Linking of sub-projects
- Monitoring budget/cashflow
- Display of a number of screens at one time
- Display a whole chart on screen
- Compatibility with main system (Ms DOS, Apple, UNIX)
- Cost
- Resource levelling
- Export to spreadsheet
- Import from older packages
- Leads and lags
- Multiple tasks
- Multiple resources
- Quick response times.

Obtain the following information from the dealer:

- What is the hardware configuration?
- What organisations are using the package? Go and see them using it. Talk to them about it.

When you've got all the information you need, refer to the sample format for evaluating proposals (Chapter 10), then set up your evaluation criteria on a spreadsheet, weight the criteria and select the best option from packages available.

Evaluating a large number of packages can be time consuming. Put the donkey work onto the seller. Give them your criteria. Let them narrow the field for you.

Whatever you choose should be easy to use, flexible and able to accommodate change easily. Our guess is that for organisational use, a simple scheduling package that can link sub-projects, and provide a spreadsheet for budget control, will meet most people's needs.

MANAGING PLANNING CHANGES ON THE COMPUTER

Your initial plan may change many times before it becomes an accurate workable document. The person doing the scheduling often has to make estimates and best guesses with regard to duration of tasks and availability of staff. Ideally this wouldn't happen. But it can, sometimes early in the piece because the team itself may not yet be assembled, or because staff may be all round the country or otherwise difficult to liaise with. So, check out assumptions and guesses with the people concerned. Most breakdowns in communication can be identified as being attributable to lack of one of those five Cs we mentioned: clarity, conciseness, completeness, correctness and courtesy. It applies to computer scheduling as much as to anything. In the following case the information was incomplete. As a result, assumptions were made that were incorrect, with serious implications.

CASE 16 — WHERE THINGS ARE NOT AS THEY SEEM!

Consultant Pauline is brought in to prepare the plan for the nation-wide project. Many areas have to be coordinated.

The draft plan is presented to the project manager and to those who will be working on the project. They are asked to check task durations and the logic.

Everyone is impressed with the chart. 'Everything is fine,' they say. Pauline checks out their optimism by asking questions. From the answers it is clear that the staff do not understand what they are looking at and, in fact, some information on the chart is not correct. Big discrepancies appear in the resource schedule — the project calendar is based on everyone working full-time, yet some of the people it turns out will be available for only a few hours a week. With Pauline checking it out at draft stage, the very unrealistic timeframe will now be corrected in the plan.

Here is another problem we came across that took a long time to figure out.

CASE 17 — THE DECIMAL POINT

This schedule incorporated many sub-projects linked to a master schedule. A number of schedulers across the country had prepared their data which was then linked to a master plan. Everything was looking good, except that the critical path wasn't showing up against expected tasks.

The team member incorporating the data was very experienced and knew the data didn't 'feel' right. He noted that the computer was showing resources as working decimal parts of days for a number of tasks. As decimal days hadn't been entered, the computer was converting the entered data for some reason.

Five hours later, after trying everything, this experienced operator finally saw the light: different people had prepared the data, so could the settings on their version of the software differ in some way? That was it! One calendar had been set differently from the rest. It showed a nine-hour day while all the other settings were for eight hours.

An inexperienced scheduler would not have known anything was wrong with the information. A few points can be taken from the case. Firstly, don't rely too heavily on computer data. It can be wrong. Secondly, use your own common sense about durations of tasks and the logic links. If it feels wrong or looks wrong, it most probably is.

HOW TO PREPARE YOUR DATA

Data is prepared manually first as shown in Chapter 6. The information is then entered on the computer. You will have coded your tasks for the following reasons:

- People can refer to the codes when changes are needed
- Codes are easy to use when you are choosing and sorting data for reports. For example, you tell the computer to sort tasks by say, alphabetical ordering, or just A to C, etc.
- People can see at a glance the tasks they are responsible for.

Schedule charts may be placed on the wall for easy reference. Amendments can be made on the chart using coloured pens — red for deletion, green for insert. Unless there are major changes during the project, once a week should be sufficient for updating on the computer. We stress the need here to back up each version of your computer project planning model before any change is made. Make sure also to title and date your changes clearly. Reconstruction costs too much in time. Always be prepared with updated information for reports and meetings. If charts have to be changed before meetings, give yourself plenty of time. Changes often generate other changes.

If you are amending a master schedule that affects the tasks within a sub-project, remember to print the affected areas and present them to the people concerned. You can imagine the chaos that might ensue if some involved people are working from different or outdated data.

Always time and date your work — a ground rule that can save considerable confusion and misunderstanding.

Keep your schedules simple for presentation to senior staff. They are interested only in key data. As a rule of thumb, restrict the tasks to no more than 20.

Computer literacy is an essential skill in project management. We pity the staff member new to both computers and project scheduling. If you are facing this difficulty, particularly as a project manager, recruit a staff member with computer know-how while you develop your own skill.

Afterword

All that is needed now is a word or two to the readers who are working in projects or interested in being part of project management. We hope that you will have read our book right through and that from now on you will keep it within hand's reach. Our major hope is that what we have put in this book will enable you to take your place as an informed and therefore valuable member of any project team at the level of your own competence. We both wish we could protect you from the school of hard knocks. We can't. Just don't make the same mistake twice. Your reward is experience. It's a pearl without price. It gives you bargaining power for your own services, and looks good on your curriculum vitae.

So, good luck in project management. We wish you success and satisfaction in your career.

Glossary

Activity   An individual work item that must be done in order to complete a project; synonymous with task.

Activity trap   Where the workers are engaged in coping with crisis activities and there is little real progress.

Allocation   The act of designating resources or tasks.

Brainstorming   Generating as many ideas as possible. The rules of brainstorming are numerous (e.g. no comment may be made on an individual's suggestion by other members of the team until all ideas are collected). The ideas generated are evaluated and those not considered worthy of further consideration are eliminated.

Communication strategy   Setting out who gets what information when, and by what means.

Communications matrix   Setting out in chart form who gets what information.

Constraints   What you get when you take into account resource limitations.

Consultant   A person who is an advisor or 'expert' on a particular topic.

Contract   An agreement between two or more parties.

Core team   People who assist at the pre-planning phase.

Cost-benefit analysis   A method used to aid decision-making by measuring costs versus benefits.

Critical path method (CPM)   A project management method of calculating the total duration of a project based upon individual task durations and dependencies. This method is the fundamental scheduling method used in many project management software packages.

Critical task   A task on the critical path. A critical task has no slack time and cannot be delayed without delaying the project completion date.

Debugging   Correcting faults in a computer program.

Dependency   A timing relationship between two tasks. For example, if one task must be completed before the other can begin, a 'finish-to-start' dependency would exist.

Duration   The expected time required to complete a task.

Elapsed duration   The total calendar time, including non-working time and holidays, between the beginning and end of work on a task.

Environment   Areas external to the project.

Escalation price   One that includes allowances for cost increases caused by general inflation during the course of the project.

Feasibility study   A detailed investigation and analysis conducted to determine the financial, technical, or other viability of a proposed project.

Fixed price contract   A contract defining precisely the scope of the work for which a fixed price or fee has been negotiated.

Gantt chart   A view that shows tasks scheduled over time. A Gantt chart shows tasks start and finish dates as well as critical and non-critical tasks.

Key tasks   Main tasks which often contain other tasks.

Lag time   A delay between two tasks that have a dependency.

Logic   Sequence of tasks determined by the order in which they should be done.

Maintenance period   A period following completion of a project during which the consultant or contractor is responsible for the correction of any faults.

Management by project   Style of management that achieves organisational objectives by means of project techniques and strategies.

Master plan   A plan of key tasks, including sub-projects.

Master schedule   A schedule of resource use across an organisation.

Matrix structure   Format that shows the use of people across work areas.

Milestone   An activity that represents a significant point in the project.

Negotiated contract   A form of contract where a price for work is negotiated by the client with the consultant.

Network analysis   A generic term for several project planning methods of which the best known is 'critical path'.

Networking   Making contact with people in various areas to share knowledge and experience.

Output   Key outcome within a main project objective.

Output manager   See 'Project director'.

People skill   Ability to 'get on' with people.

Post-project review   A report which reviews the project and records information for future use.

Predecessor   A task that must start or finish before another task can start.

Project   Work which has a beginning and an end.

Project brief   Concentrates on objectives; starts off as a terms of reference, ends up as a working guide.

Project director   'Owner' of a project.

Project hierarchy   Levels of people involved in the project.

Project leader   A person who manages a sub-project.

Project management   A technique based on objectives used to manage, plan, monitor and control a project.

Project manager   A person who is responsible for taking the project to a successful conclusion.

Project team   Skilled people employed to carry out the project tasks.

Proposal analysis matrix   A method for analysing proposals.

Quality control group   A group of people who oversee the quality output of a project. Some groups have authority; others are advisory only.

Resource   Anything that is essential for the completion of a task: people, money, equipment, time.

Retentions   Money withheld to cover the cost of remedying any defects.

Scale of fees   Usually quoted in consultants' proposals. It covers the range of fees charged by that company for their staff.

Schedule   A plan that shows tasks, timing, dependencies and milestones of a project.

Slack time   The difference between the time available for a task to be completed and the duration of a task.

Software   The programmes that tell a computer what to do.

Scope of work (specification)   A comprehensive description and explanation of the project, its components and materials and the required standard of work.

Spreadsheet   A matrix of cells that can be mathematically linked to each other.

Steering committee   See 'Quality control group'.

Sub-project   A portion of a larger project with its own leader.

Task   A unit of work. A project is made up of a series of tasks.

Technocrat   A person who believes technology has all the answers.

Terms of reference   Contains expectations of the project 'owner'.

Timeframe   The duration of time allowed for a project or part of the project.

Variations   Additions to or subtractions from the scope of work in the contract or brief.

Recommended reading

Austen, A and Neale, R (eds) (1986) *Managing Construction Projects*, International Labour Office, Geneva.

Buzan, T (1974) *Use Your Head*, BBC Publications.

Fisher, R and Ury, W (1982) *Getting to Yes*, Hutchinson.

Francis, D (1989) *Organizational Communication*, Gower Business Skills.

Garrett, B (1987) *The Learning Organisation*, Fontana.

Janis, I (1972) *Victims of Groupthink*, Houghton Mifflin.

Meyers, G and Holusha, J (1988) *Managing Crisis*, Underhill.

Michael, N (1988) *How to Say What You Mean*, Heinemann Reed.

Rawlinson, J (1986) *Creative Thinking and Brainstorming*, Gower.

Sligo, F (1990) *Conflict Management*, GP Books.

Svantesson, I (1989) *Mind Mapping and Memory*, Swan.

Sweet, P (1989) *Report Writing*, GP Books.

Weiss, D (1988) *Creative Problem Solving*, Weiss.

OTHER BOOKS BY KOGAN PAGE

Andersen, E, Grude, K, Haug, T and Turner, J (1989) *Goal Directed Project Management*, Kogan Page.

Davies, M (1992) *Project Management* (Workshop Package), Kogan Page.

Haynes, M (1990) *Project Management: From Idea to Implementation*, Kogan Page.

Lashbrooke, G (1992) *A Project Manager's Handbook*, Kogan Page.

Career development

Certification in project management can be gained through:

> The Association of Project Managers (UK)
> 85 Oxford Rd
> High Wycombe
> Bucks HP11 2DX
> Tel: 0494 440090
> Fax: 0494 528937

Graduate courses are offered by:

> The Project Management Institute
> PO Box 189
> Webster N C 28788
> USA
> Tel: (734) 227 7401

Index